I read this book in one sitting. After 30 years across
GTM, this book opens your eyes to change that m[
With AI accelerating buyer behavior and collapsing traditional funnels,
the shift from Sales-Led and Product-Led to Market-Led is no longer
optional – it's urgent. *Market-Led Growth* offers tangible actions you
can take immediately to impact, grow, and even save your business. It
doesn't just explain the shift – it gives you the playbook. A must-read
for any leader building a responsive, customer-obsessed organization.

**Robbie Traube**,
President and Chief Customer Officer, Zuora

People talk of painkillers or vitamins, well, Felix's book is the Valium
for modern founders desperately seeking and trying to hold onto PMF.
The realization that PMF is a process and not a destination is profound
and mirrors exactly what we all see in the market. We are all living in
a time of massive innovation and low barriers to entry. Only the most
agile companies will thrive, and those without a growth culture, as
described by Felix, will not be here for long. I loved this book, and it
landed with me just when I needed it most.

**Barrie Hadfield**,
Founder and CEO, Mindset AI

Felix's work is not just a reflection on where we've been but a roadmap
for where we're going. It's a must-read for anyone serious about
building businesses that can thrive in the age of AI.

**Dominic Cameron**,
Ex-CTO PhotoBox, LastMinute.com, ITV.com

Felix deftly exposes the fault lines inherent in product-centric operating
models – fault lines that we have all sensed but struggled to name.
Fractures that the new AI economic logic is ruthlessly widening on a
daily basis. Then, he hands you the roadmap to fix them. With sharp
clarity and practical logic, he shows what every organization must do
to change at speed, how to lead the execution, and how to use metrics
to drive the cultural shift we all need. This is the most urgent and

relevant book I have read in years. I had set a meeting to discuss the implications before I was even halfway through. This isn't just a book that delivers insights; it's a book that demands action.

**Susie Buckridge**,
CEO of TalkTalk

This book doesn't just critique the old models – it replaces them. *Market-Led Growth* shows how to rewire your GTM engine around signal, speed, and adaptability. It's already changed how I think about org design, planning cycles, and what 'customer-centric' really means. Essential reading for any exec trying to future-proof their business.

**Jim Selman**,
Ex-MD of Allison Worldwide

Felix Danczak has written the GTM blueprint for the AI era. *Market Led Growth* doesn't just predict the future of go-to-market, it gives operators a way to survive and win in it.

**Yoni Benshaul**,
Founder and CEO of Dreamhub.ai

Felix Danczak

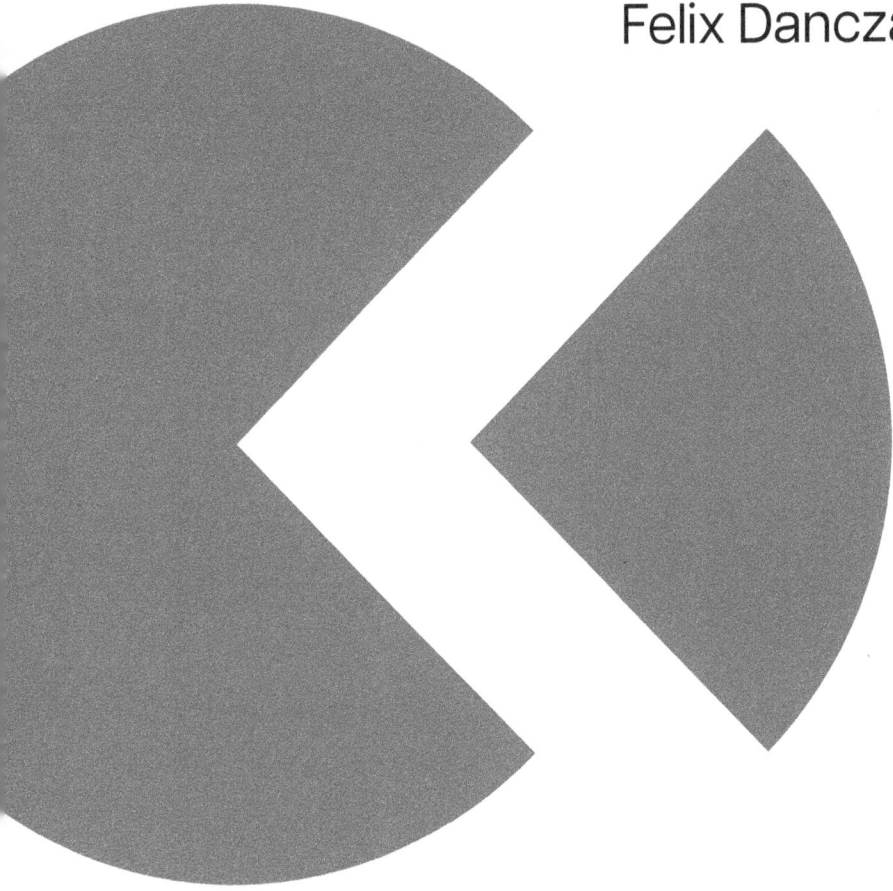

# Market-led growth

## A NEW OPERATING SYSTEM FOR BUSINESS IN THE AGE OF AI

First published in Great Britain by Practical Inspiration Publishing, 2026

ISBN    978-1-78860-915-9 (paperback)
        978-1-78860-914-2 (hardback)
        978-1-78860-916-6 (epub)

EU GPSR representative: LOGOS EUROPE, 9 rue Nicolas Poussin, LA ROCHELLE 17000, France Contact@logoseurope.eu

Want to bulk-buy copies of this book for your team and colleagues? We can customize the content and co-brand *Market-Led Growth* to suit your business's needs.

Please email info@practicalinspiration.com for more details.

Practical Inspiration
Publishing

# Dedication

To those who encouraged me every step – Abby, Adam, Alfie, Darian, James H, Jamie W, Jenny, Julian, and Rosie – thank you. Whether through patience or belief or reading parts of this in draft, you kept me going when I was distracted, obsessed, or unsure of what I was building.

To Ryan and Kenta – the best editors I could have asked for. To Evan, without whose design-brain none of my ideas would make sense. To those who inspire me – everyone who built Zephr, and then my marketing mob at Zuora who were the best team a person could ever hope to lead (and to whom I can only say 'this is the way').

A special thank you to Joelle Kaufman – this book would still be a half-baked idea in the back of my head if it weren't for your clarity, challenge, and generosity. You've been the best sounding board, coach, and thought partner I could have ever hoped for.

And to little Arlo. It'll be your world soon enough – I hope you find it as exciting as I do.

*Never doubt that a small group of talented people can change the world – it's the only thing that ever has.*

**Margaret Mead**

# Contents

## Part I: Where we are, why we're here, and where we're going

## Part II: Inside the Market-Led Growth operating system

## Part III: Implementing Market-Led Growth

# Abbreviations

| | |
|---|---|
| AI | artificial intelligence |
| API | application programming interface |
| ARR | annual recurring revenue |
| ASP | average selling price |
| | |
| B2B | business-to-business |
| | |
| CAC | customer acquisition costs |
| CPC | cost-per-click |
| CPG | consumer-packaged-goods |
| CPL | cost-per-lead |
| CRM | customer relationship management |
| CSM | customer success manager |
| | |
| DM | direct message |
| DSO | dynamic shared ownership |
| | |
| EMEA | Europe, the Middle East and Africa |
| | |
| FYR | failure yield ratio |
| | |
| GenAI | generative AI |
| GTM | go-to-market |
| | |
| ICP | ideal customer profile |
| | |
| LLM | large language models |
| LTV | life-time value |
| | |
| MAS | market activation speed |
| MLG | Market-Led Growth |
| | |
| NRR | net retained revenue |
| | |
| OS | operating system |

| | |
|---|---|
| P&L | profit and loss |
| PE | private equity |
| PLG | Product-Led Growth |
| PMF | product-market fit |
| QBR | quarterly business review |
| RPP | revenue per market pod |
| SaaS | software-as-a-service |
| SEO | search engine optimization |
| SDR | sales development representatives |
| SLG | Sales-Led Growth |
| UX | user experience |
| VC | venture capital |
| ZIRP | zero interest rate policy |

# Foreword

As someone who has navigated the tech landscape from its analog beginnings to today's AI-driven era, chairing scale-ups and startups, I've witnessed firsthand the seismic shifts in how we build and grow businesses. It astonishes me to recall my early days in computing, working with analog systems and rudimentary programming.

I remember feeding punch cards into room-sized machines, waiting hours for a single computation – a stark contrast to today's real-time processing. It was a world where software was less a product than a painstaking craft, and progress was measured in years, not milliseconds.

Business School introduced me to overnight batch processing, where results took days, not milliseconds. Technological progress was incremental, measured in years. Early software sales were dominated by a few giants like IBM, who pioneered relationship-building and storytelling – early hallmarks of Sales-Led Growth (SLG).

As a BBC executive producer in the 1980s, I saw technology transform live television production. We shifted from paper-based graphics to tools like the Quantel Paintbox, which brought computer-generated visuals to live broadcasts. Software development was still outsourced then, but we eventually embraced in-house innovation with the BBC Computer Graphics Workshop for election coverage. We marveled at the newfound speed, unaware of how much faster things would become. Product management, as we know it, was still a distant concept.

But everything was about to change. Again.

The internet revolutionized everything, from e-commerce to software development. Despite the dot-com bust, progress continued with advancements in infrastructure and coding practices, though projects still spanned months or years.

As CTOs, we balanced CEO visions with technical realities, grappling with new concepts like scalability and agility. Our approach evolved from building what we could to building what was needed, embracing data and user-centricity. Product management was emerging, but Product-Led Growth (PLG) was still on the horizon.

We learned to balance structure with flexibility, adopting cross-functional teams for faster iteration. B2B software, led by pioneers like Salesforce, relied on sales-driven growth. User-centricity was emerging but not yet central.

The 2010s saw the rise of Vertical SaaS, peaking around 2021 before market corrections and the advent of Generative AI (GenAI). Amidst this, PLG emerged as a new paradigm, exemplified by companies like Dropbox and Slack, emphasizing user-centricity and rapid iteration.

But everything was about to change. Again.

Key technologies like the internet, PCs, and smartphones laid the groundwork. Now, AI, particularly GenAI, promises to accelerate change even further, driven by consumer adoption. AI doesn't just speed up processes – it rewrites them, enabling businesses to anticipate market shifts before they fully emerge.

Yet, as Felix Danczak astutely observes in this book, even PLG is not the final destination. In a world where AI collapses feedback loops and democratizes capabilities, businesses must evolve further – to a model where the market itself dictates strategy in real-time. This is the essence of Market-Led Growth (MLG).

This book insightfully explores this evolution, advocating for MLG as the next step, where AI enhances our ability to respond to market signals with unprecedented speed. It eloquently outlines the future of software development, emphasizing verifiability, experimentation, talent optimization, and human-AI collaboration – crucial for success in the coming years.

My journey through roles in broadcasting, media, and technology leadership has given me a unique vantage point on this accelerating pace of change. This work is not just a reflection on where we've been but a roadmap for where we're going. It's a must-read for anyone serious about building businesses that can thrive in the age of AI.

I am honored to introduce this book, which captures the spirit of innovation and adaptation that has defined my career. Felix's insights are not just timely; they are essential. This is the way forward.

**Dominic Cameron**

# Introduction

Most companies will tell you they're customer-centric. That they listen to the market. That they're data-informed, agile, responsive. You and I both know that's not really true.

Inside the building, most decisions are still made based on internal priorities, historical momentum, or the loudest stakeholder in the room. Sales runs the calendar. Marketing runs the narrative. Product runs the roadmap. Everyone's fighting for headcount.

The customer becomes an abstraction ('we sell to accountants!', or 'we help digital first brands') – something we reference, but rarely actively and dynamically reorient around. Even our idea of the 'the buyer' is relatively fixed. We spend our days thinking from the inside → out.

Meanwhile something strange is happening outside. The old engines of growth are sputtering. Channels that used to print pipeline now deliver noise. Buyers are flooded with options and tuned out of traditional go-to-market (GTM) strategies. Demand is fragmented and less predictable, and AI is accelerating everything – new competitors, new interfaces, new expectations. What used to take teams now takes prompts.

AI is to the knowledge economy what the last industrial revolution was to physical labor. It's mechanizing cognition. Except this time, the machinery isn't expensive, gated, or rare. Everyone's getting their own personal steam engine on day one (a steam engine that can change shape depending on what you want it to be, minute by minute).

The consequences aren't just about productivity – they're about power, structure, and the shape of organizations themselves.

I wrote this book because the growth models of the last couple of decades – Sales-Led Growth, Product-Led Growth, even so-called 'customer-led' models – aren't built for this level of volatility. They assume a world of linear funnels, clear handoffs, and stable product-market fit (PMF). That world is gone.

In this new environment, PMF isn't a milestone – it's a moving target – Segments shift, buyer expectations evolve, competitors appear overnight, and most companies don't notice the drift until revenue softens, win rates fall, or retention starts to crack.

The companies that succeed now won't be the ones with the best branding or the most aggressive sales teams. They'll be the ones tracking fit at the most granular level – sensing where value is shifting, and continuously adapting how they position, package, and deliver what they offer. Fit is no longer something you find. It's something you have to *keep*.

This book is for founders, executives, operators, and investors who are trying to build companies that can grow in a world where the ground keeps shifting. It's especially urgent for those at the center of the vortex – software companies, software-as-a-service (SaaS) platforms, digital-first services, content production – where scale was built on assumptions that no longer hold.

But even those further from the center – expert networks, media firms, recruitment, or education – aren't immune. Even manufacturing and logistics are being impacted. The closer your value lies to knowledge work, the faster your time runs out.

Where you sit determines how fast you must move. But make no mistake: the logic of growth has changed. This book is about what comes next. What replaces it is not just a new set of tactics. It's a new orientation – one that puts the market at the center of how you build, fund, organize, and scale. I call it *Market-Led Growth*. It's not a shiny new playbook or a rebrand of what you're already doing. It's a different way of operating: more adaptive, more decentralized, and more aligned with the market, day to day.

It's a guide to rethinking how your company works – from how you gather intelligence, to how you organize teams, to how you resource initiatives and learn what's working. Yes, there will be some frameworks (useful ones, I hope). But the goal is simpler: to help you operate in sync with a market that won't sit still.

## What you'll learn

This book isn't just about naming the problem, it's about helping you build a business that can grow in a fundamentally new market. Across three parts, you'll learn:

- **Why the old models are breaking** – and why this isn't just a tactical failure, but a deeper misalignment between how companies are built and how markets behave.
- **How to sense and respond to demand in real time** – using a mix of AI-native systems and human judgment to cut through noise and act on signal.
- **How to structure your company for speed, learning, and adaptability** – from decentralized execution pods to market-aligned incentives and dynamic resourcing.
- **What leadership looks like when there are no fixed maps** – and how to lead an organization designed for continuous movement, not static plans.

This is *not* a book with 'one weird trick' for boosting pipeline. It's not about hacking your CAC-to-LTV ratio (your cost to acquire a customer – compared to their life-time value to your business) for better metrics next quarter. If you want that, you'll need to read something else.

Instead, think of it as an operating manual for Market-Led Growth: not a one-size-fits-all playbook, but a new way of building around signal, responsiveness, and velocity. The companies that thrive in this next era won't be the ones that grow the fastest. They'll be the ones that reinvent the fastest. This book is a call to rebuild – from the outside in.

**Felix Danczak**

August 2025

# Part I

# Where we are, why we're here, and where we're going

# 1

# A new game has begun

Something fundamental has changed. Revenue is harder to grow. Customers are harder to reach. Marketing channels that once scaled easily are stalling. Sales cycles are lengthening. Unit economics that once passed board scrutiny are now triggering hard conversations. Across industries, leaders are experiencing a common frustration: the same strategies that once delivered predictable growth no longer work the way they used to.

This is not a temporary disruption, it's not a market cycle or a blip in buyer behavior, it's a structural transition. Three foundational forces are converging – each powerful, but which together form a new baseline for how businesses operate, grow, and survive.

First, the rise of AI represents more than a technological leap. It is the beginning of a new industrial era, one that reshapes the economics of knowledge work, the speed of execution, and the lifespan of competitive advantage. Second, the era of cheap capital is over. Zero interest rate policy (ZIRP) created a decade-long distortion in growth expectations, funding inefficient models and masking their weaknesses. That financial regime has ended, and with it, the tolerance for business models that cannot self-sustain. Third, customer demand has fragmented beyond recognition. What was once a mass market is now a mosaic of niche audiences, decentralized decision-making, and trust-based ecosystems.

Individually, any one of these trends would challenge the assumptions most businesses are built on. Together, they are redefining the conditions for growth. The organizations that continue to treat them as background noise – or worse, as short-term headwinds to 'ride out' – are misreading the moment. The old game is over. A new one has begun.

## This is not just another cycle

Business leaders are used to operating within cycles – of growth and correction, boom and retrenchment. Most executive teams have weathered downturns before. They understand how to trim costs, shift messaging, or reallocate budget. They know how to 'optimize' their way through turbulence. But what's happening now is not turbulence.

The dominant models of the last two decades – Sales-Led Growth (SLG) and Product-Led Growth (PLG) worked because the conditions around them supported their logic. SLG scaled in a world of long sales cycles, risk-averse buyers, and predictable procurement processes. PLG thrived when customer acquisition was cheap, viral loops could be engineered, and distribution was winner-take-most. Both models assumed a relatively stable environment: find product-market fit (PMF), build a go-to-market (GTM) engine around it, and scale with discipline. The engine could be tweaked, tuned, and optimized, but its structure remained fundamentally the same.

The assumptions that underpinned scale – cheap capital, consistent buyer behavior, reliable acquisition channels – are no longer reliable. In their place is something faster, more fragmented, and far less forgiving. Capital has become expensive and cautious. Buyers are harder to reach, harder to convert, and less willing to commit. Entire channels are shifting beneath marketers' feet, often without warning. Even successful companies are finding that what worked last year now delivers diminishing returns – or no returns at all.

What's breaking down is not just execution, it's strategy. Because the change is *structural* – not cyclical – it is difficult to respond with incremental adjustments. Leaders continue to revise their campaigns, restructure their teams, and re-forecast their numbers, without confronting the deeper problem: the rules of the game have changed, and the playbook hasn't.

The three key trends that sit beneath this shifting sand are not equal – one will have far bigger and longer-reaching effects. But we need to understand them all to understand the terrain on which we are now playing our game. They are:

1. AI driven disruption;
2. Post ZIRP financial pressure; and
3. Hyper fragmentation of consumer demand.

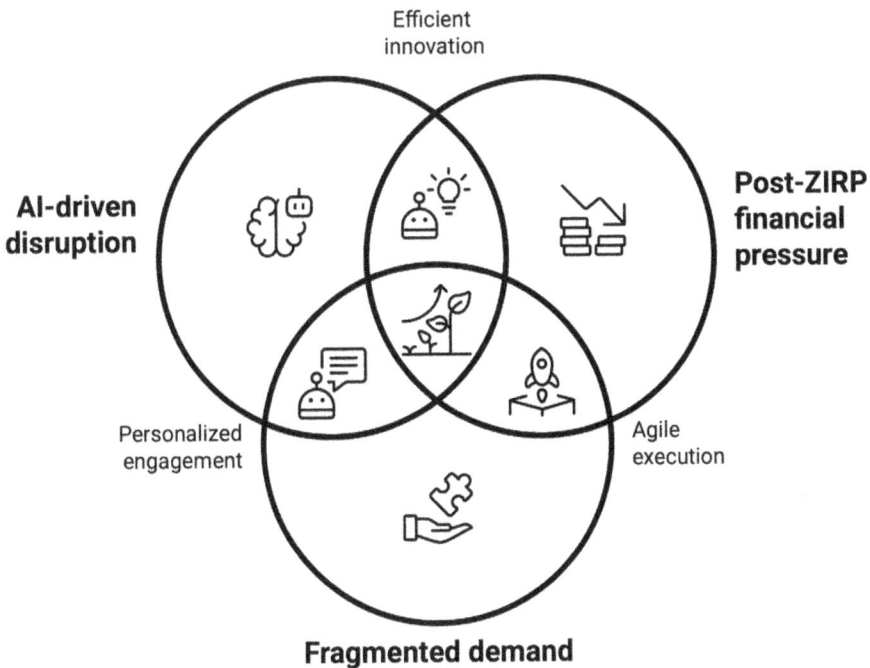

**Figure 1** The new conditions for growth. AI disruption, financial pressure, and fragmented demand are reshaping growth. Winning now means innovating efficiently, executing fast, and engaging personally.

## Section 1: The AI industrial revolution

For over a century, the growth model of modern business has followed a familiar pattern. Capital enables scale. Scale delivers efficiency. Efficiency creates margin. Margin funds further growth. This cycle – capital → scale → efficiency → profit – has been the operating logic behind industrial expansion, startup financing, public-market valuations, and corporate planning. It is so deeply embedded in business language that we treat its assumptions as laws of nature. We speak of 'economies of scale,' and 'efficiency gains,' as if they were eternal truths.

AI is challenging this basic industrial model. AI is not just a tool – it's a new industrial substrate. Like steam, electricity, or the microchip before it, *AI represents a true industrial revolution*. But unlike its predecessors – which mechanized physical labor or accelerated computation – AI directly targets knowledge work. It automates the work of analysts, marketers, designers, coders, and operators. It alters not just how work gets done, but who does it, how fast, and at what cost. As it does, *it begins to unravel the industrial logic that once linked investment, scale, and return.*

### AI makes capital intensity less predictive

First, AI challenges the logic of scale. In traditional business logic, more capital meant more headcount, more reach, more capacity. But in an AI-native environment, that link weakens. A small team with the right tooling can produce code, content, strategy, and analytics at the same throughput – and often higher quality – than a much larger one operating under legacy workflows. The marginal return on capital becomes uneven and unpredictable. Spending more doesn't reliably produce more. In many cases, it simply adds friction. Just because you raised lots of money, is no guarantee of your success.

### Scale doesn't guarantee efficiency

Second, scale is now *inversely* related to efficiency. The entire concept of 'efficiencies of scale' assumed that larger operations could reduce marginal cost through repetition, specialization, and infrastructure leverage. But AI tools don't need to be trained in the same way humans do, and they don't take time to replicate. They scale instantly. They improve continuously. In many organizations, adding human-scale now introduces coordination drag and slows execution. In AI-era operations, smaller teams often outperform larger ones not because they have more capacity, but because they have fewer bottlenecks.

## The product lifecycle is collapsing, and the moat is filling in

Third, efficiency no longer guarantees profit. This one is *really* scary – not because efficiency is irrelevant, but because the conditions required to turn it into margin have eroded. In many knowledge-heavy sectors, *AI is accelerating the collapse of product moats*. Features can be copied. Workflows can be cloned. Microsoft reports that 30% of all of its code is now AI-generated.[1] The traditional product lifecycle – build, grow, harvest – has compressed. Differentiation now decays in weeks, not years. This undermines the entire logic of delayed monetization.

Companies built to 'scale now, profit later' increasingly find that 'later' never arrives. Their maturity phase gets preempted by competitors and the subsequent race to the bottom before they can recoup the investment made during growth. A startup that launches a novel capability today cannot hold on to that competitive advantage to scale. Competitors can reverse-engineer, replicate, and relaunch a similar experience at near-zero marginal cost. What once required deep engineering resources can now be mimicked with the right prompt, an open-source model, and an integration layer.

---

[1] Satya Nadella, interview by Mark Zuckerberg, *CNBC*, April 29, 2025, www.cnbc.com/2025/04/29/satya-nadella-says-as-much-as-30percent-of-microsoft-code-is-written-by-ai.html

## Efficiency doesn't guarantee profit, or even survival

But the problem runs deeper. Efficiency itself can become a liability. Organizations that optimize too aggressively around fixed workflows, fixed products, or fixed roles in order to reduce cost often lose their capacity to adapt. The very systems that once made them fast and lean now make them rigid. In a volatile market, this rigidity becomes fatal. Revenue doesn't flow to the company with the lowest cost structure – it flows to the one that can respond fastest to shifting demand. That requires slack, experimentation, and the willingness to deviate from the process in real time. Efficiency is the enemy of that agility.

## AI is rewriting the growth and retention model

This breakdown is not theoretical. It is already visible in how competitive advantage erodes, how margins compress, and how quickly previously successful strategies begin to stall. AI is not just automating tasks – it is reshaping every input, pathway, and constraint that modern growth models were built on.

None of this means that growth is impossible. But in industries where knowledge work is central, growth must now be earned through continuous alignment with the market. The winners are not the most *efficient* operators. They are the most *adaptive* ones.

- **AI is replacing the search engine**
  - AI-powered search assistants are making search engine optimization (SEO), content marketing, and pay-per click-based demand capture dramatically less effective. Buyers no longer click through ten blue links. They ask a question – and get a direct answer. If your product isn't in that summary, you don't exist. For companies that built their GTM strategy on capturing inbound traffic, this is an existential disruption.
- **AI is automating GTM execution**
  - Sales prospecting, email sequencing, ad optimization, campaign management – tasks once handled by full

teams – are now being automated at scale. AI sales development representatives (SDRs) qualify leads. Large language models (LLMs) generate content. Pricing assistants run dynamic discounting models. Execution speed is no longer determined by headcount – it's determined by infrastructure.

- **PMF is no longer a destination**
  - ○ In the old model, you found PMF, locked it in, and scaled. Now, PMF mutates. Fast. AI shortens feedback loops and accelerates imitation. Fit is no longer something you reach. It's something you *maintain* – by evolving faster than your environment.
- **The product itself is becoming fluid**
  - ○ Products are shifting from packaged to adaptive. From 'shipped features' to 'configurable experiences.' The product no longer ends at the release. It lives, adjusts, reconfigures itself in real time. Customers expect this. AI makes it possible. The companies that thrive will be those that design their product systems – and their teams – to mutate continuously, not incrementally.
- **AI is collapsing switching cost, challenging retention models**
  - ○ AI is driving down the cost of change. It can translate systems, migrate workflows, and reconstruct interfaces with minimal effort. The barriers that once made switching slow, expensive, or risky are dissolving. As a result, retention is no longer a function of inertia. It's a function of value, responsiveness, and clarity. In a world where leaving is easy, staying has to be worth it. Moats must now be built on momentum, not entrenchment.

## A new economic logic requires a new operating model

The old industrial model treated growth as a linear function of capital: raise money, build scale, extract efficiency, harvest profit. AI

**Old industrial model**

**AI-native model**

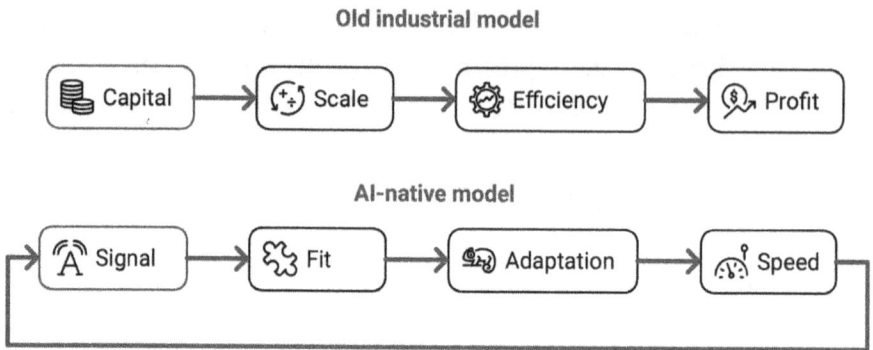

**Figure 2** Old versus new operating models. Legacy models move linearly. AI-native models loop continuously – learning, adapting, and accelerating with each cycle.

is unravelling that logic. In its place, a new loop is emerging – one that begins not with capital, but with *signal*. The companies that thrive now are those that detect shifts early, respond with speed, adapt continuously, and stay aligned with where the market is going. This is not a straight line, it's a loop, as shown in Figure 2.

Fit generates traction, but the loop never ends because the moment you have fit, the market will adapt with immediate competition and changed consumer desires. In an AI-native economy, advantage flows to reflexes, not resources.

We'll return to the implications of this shift throughout the book. But for now, we need to look at a second foundational change – one that has removed the financial cushion many companies once relied on: the end of cheap capital.

## Section 2: Post-ZIRP financial pressure

For over a decade, the business world operated under an extraordinary financial regime – one that most leaders grew accustomed to, but few fully understood. Near-zero interest rates, abundant venture funding, and a risk-on investor mindset created conditions in which capital was not just available but cheap to the point of distortion. In this environment, efficiency became optional.

Growth became the imperative, not efficiency. Entire operating models were built on the assumption that money would always be there to fund the next phase. This was the ZIRP era, it wasn't normal, it just lasted long enough to feel that way and it skewed a lot of assumptions for leaders who 'came of age' during this period.

## ZIRP wasn't normal – it just felt like it

During the 2010s, capital flowed into startups and growth-stage companies at unprecedented volumes and on increasingly generous terms. The expectation was clear: grow quickly, capture market share, worry about profitability later. The phrase 'go-to-market' came to mean 'burn to acquire,' and the burn was justified by a simple narrative: scale would eventually fix the unit economics.

This is the macroeconomic environment that shaped – and in many cases, solidified – today's dominant growth models. SLG assumed that high acquisition costs could be absorbed so long as customer lifetime value was strong. PLG thrived on the assumption that distribution could be scaled virally and monetized later. Even the pursuit of PMF was treated as a phase that could be extended indefinitely, provided capital kept coming.

The problem is not that these ideas were illogical, it's that they were subsidized by a financial climate that no longer exists.

## The financial environment has flipped

We are now in the opposite regime. Interest rates have risen. Inflation is non-trivial. Public markets have repriced risk, and private capital has followed. Investors are no longer rewarding growth at all costs. They are demanding clear paths to profitability – and in many cases, immediate proof of high operating leverage. Metrics that were once treated as secondary (burn rate, CAC payback, gross margin) are now gating criteria for funding. In 2018, a company with US$5–10 million in revenue, decent growth, and a burn multiple of 3x – meaning it was spending US$3 in operating losses for every US$1 of new revenue – could raise a healthy Series C round. Today, that same profile might not even get a first meeting.

This change is not temporary, it reflects a reassessment of risk tolerance across the capital stack. Growth is no longer inherently valuable, it must be efficient, sustainable, and justifiable on a per-dollar basis, and that shift has profound implications for how companies go to market.

## When capital was cheap, bad economics could hide

For over a decade, the cost of capital masked the fragility of many growth models. Sales-led businesses could justify ballooning CACs because future LTVs were treated as guaranteed. Product-led companies could defer monetization for years, banking on eventual dominance. Even flawed unit economics were tolerated – because capital was cheap, abundant, and patient.

Today, every dollar is being asked to prove itself. High burn isn't a sign of ambition – it's a sign of inefficiency. Long payback periods aren't strategic – they're disqualifying. The very financial scaffolding that supported these models – debt-funded headcount, marketing overspend, multi-year losses – is no longer structurally viable.

This shift isn't philosophical, it's mathematical. When capital costs rise, so does the opportunity cost of delayed return. Investors no longer believe that scale alone will fix the model. They're asking a different question now: not 'How big can this get?' but 'Can this pay back?'.

Many of the dominant GTM playbooks of the last decade are buckling – not because they were poorly run, but because they were built for a world where capital was artificially cheap. The result is a reckoning. Not just with tactics – but with the economics they depended on. Cheap capital didn't just fuel growth. It distorted the cost of it.

## The marginal dollar must now justify itself

This is not just a matter of investor mood, it's a fundamental change to how resource allocation is being managed across organizations. CFOs are no longer asking how fast a team can scale – they're asking what the return is on the next dollar of spend. Boards are shifting incentives accordingly. GTM leaders are finding that ambition alone no longer warrants budget. Cost-efficiency is no longer optional. Every spend must be tied to a credible path to margin.

This doesn't mean growth is over. But it does mean that growth must now compete directly with profitability for prioritization. The marginal dollar is no longer defaulted to acquisition, it is allocated, scrutinized, and expected to deliver.

## The safety net is gone

The effect of ZIRP was not just financial, it was psychological, it created a buffer – a sense that mistakes could be paid for with the next raise or debt issue, that GTM inefficiencies were temporary, that scaling before refining was an acceptable trade. That buffer is gone.

The companies that survive this phase won't be the ones that raise the most, or hire the fastest. They will be the ones that realign their operating models to a world where capital is once again a constraint. Where high cash burn without good reason is not a sign of ambition, but a measure of failure. Where strategic clarity and operational discipline become prerequisites for funding, not outcomes of it.

## What comes next

First, AI broke the logic of production. Now, the end of cheap capital is breaking the logic of funding. The next section looks at the third and final force reshaping modern growth: demand itself. The buyer has changed too – and this is undermining the once predictable, monolithic market.

## Section 3: The fragmentation of demand

For years, growth strategy has relied on a coherent view of the market: that there is a definable buyer, reachable through predictable channels, who moves through a logical sequence of awareness, evaluation, and purchase. This premise underpins the idea of the funnel, it assumes centralization – of media, of messaging, of decision-making authority – and it assumes that with the right campaign, the right content, and the right timing, demand can be systematically generated and converted. That model is falling apart.

### The funnel has fractured

The funnel was never a perfect representation of buyer behavior, but it was directionally useful. It reflected a world where buyers were accessible through shared platforms – trade publications, conferences, analyst reports, outbound email, paid media. Marketing owned the top of the funnel, sales managed the middle, and customer success handled retention and expansion. The edges blurred, but the model held because demand itself was relatively centralized.

Today, that centralization is gone. Buyers don't follow a linear path. They don't rely on vendor-controlled content to educate themselves. They don't wait for a sales rep to initiate a conversation. Instead, they operate inside decentralized, often invisible networks. Product recommendations happen in Slack groups, WhatsApp threads, Discord communities, and private direct messages (DMs) – well outside the visibility or influence of a company's GTM infrastructure. Buying criteria are shaped by peers, operators, micro-influencers, and AI-generated summaries – not by brochures or nurture sequences. In many cases, buyers evaluate entire categories without ever filling out a form or taking a call.

To make matters worse, the once-cheap distribution channels many firms relied on – SEO, app stores, viral loops – now demand real spend to compete, with increasingly marginal returns. With dozens of competitors targeting every overlapping niche, the price of digital ads has spiked. Cost-per-click (CPC) climbed approximately 34% between 2022 and 2024,[2] and in the 12 months to June 2025, cost-per-lead (CPL) rose by an average of 19% (and far greater in areas with high competition – upwards of 130% in Entertainment).[3] Yet, as these channels falter, businesses reflexively just shovel more money into them. One consultancy estimated that in 2024, companies globally spent 13% more on digital ads, yet conversion rates dropped 6%.[4]

When discovery, evaluation, and decision-making happen away from a company's owned channels – or outside its field of view entirely – the traditional levers of influence weaken. Just as important, the signals disappear. The telemetry that GTM teams once relied on – web traffic, form fills, content views, event attendance, sales interactions – no longer provides a reliable picture of intent. Demand may still be shifting, but companies find out only *long* after it has moved.

When you can't see where interest is forming, how priorities are evolving, or which narratives are resonating, you lose the ability to adapt in time. Visibility isn't a luxury – it's the precondition for responsiveness – and it's evaporating.

## Buyers expect flexibility, not process

In parallel, buyer expectations have changed, it's not just that buyers consume information differently – it's that they expect to operate

---

[2] HockeyStack Labs. 2025. 'Google Ads Benchmarks from 2022 to 2024.' Last modified June 2025. www.hockeystack.com/lab-blog-posts/google-ads-benchmarks-from-2022-to-2024

[3] WordStream by LOCALiQ. 2022. '2022 Search Advertising Benchmarks for Every Industry.' *WordStream Blog*, last modified June 11, 2025, www.wordstream.com/blog/ws/2022/11/10/search-advertising-benchmarks

[4] Okoone. 2024. 'Businesses Are Spending More on Digital Ads, But Converting Less.' *Okoone Spark*, February 10, 2025, www.okoone.com/spark/marketing-growth/businesses-are-spending-more-on-digital-ads-but-converting-less/

on their own terms. They want to self-educate, explore options asynchronously, and trial products without going through a prescribed flow. This shift is often misunderstood as a call for more PLG, but that misses the point. What buyers want is *control* – control over how they engage, how quickly they move, and which paths they take.

This puts pressure on any GTM model that assumes sequencing, gating, or handoffs. SLG motions that rely on staged qualification and multi-week nurturing cycles often feel slow and intrusive. PLG flows that presume a smooth progression from usage to monetization break down when buyer needs shift mid-cycle or when value isn't obvious immediately. In both cases, rigidity fails. GTM execution must become more fluid – less focused on pushing buyers through a pre-chosen model and more focused on meeting them where they already are.

This doesn't mean abandoning structure, it means building systems that are responsive by default. Where customer behavior informs the path, not the other way around.

## From standardized products to personalized services

This expectation of responsiveness isn't unique to business-to-business (B2B). It reflects a deeper, long-running shift across industries: the movement from standardized products to personalized services. It's a pattern we've seen before.

In the early stages of any industry, products tend to be rigid and uniform – not because companies want them that way, but because scale and technology constraints leave little choice. Users must adapt to the product. Over time, as industries mature and capabilities improve, the dynamic flips: products adapt to users. Flexibility becomes the differentiator. Responsiveness becomes the expectation.

Telephony is a clear example. Landlines were static, standardized, and dictated behavior. Families placed them on dedicated tables in high-traffic areas of the home. Making a call meant going to the phone – on its terms. Mobile phones began to change that. Smartphones completed the transformation. Today, your phone is an extension of your preferences: custom apps, ringtones, filters, and notification rules. The user shapes the experience, not the manufacturer.

The same pattern reshaped television. From rigid broadcast schedules to DVRs to AI-personalized streaming libraries, each stage moved control from the provider to the viewer. No two Netflix homepages are alike – not because Netflix knows what content you need, but because it has learned how to adapt to what you want.

Almost every knowledge-work heavy industry is now undergoing the same transition. What once passed as 'product' is now expected to behave like a service, from media to medicine: adaptive, contextual, and responsive. Buyers don't want to be sold a fixed solution. They expect tools that evolve with their needs, respond to their behavior, and flex to their environment. GTM models built for standardized offerings no longer map to this reality. They assume consistency where variation is now the norm.

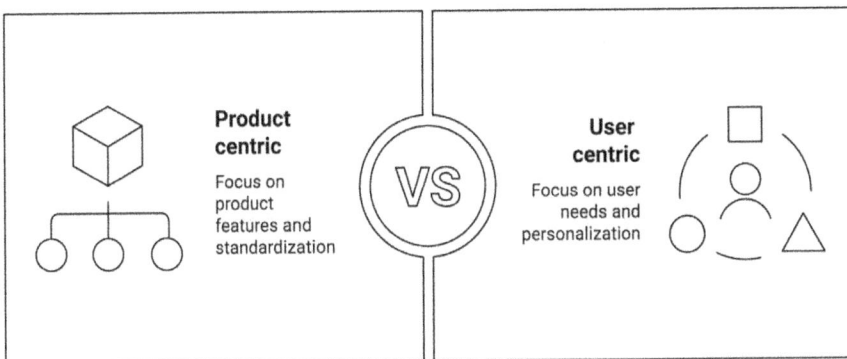

**Figure 3** From standardized products to personalized services. The shift from product-centric to user-centric models reflects a broader move from feature-driven standardization to needs-based personalization.

## Segmentation is self-directed

The fragmentation of demand doesn't just break the funnel – it breaks segmentation. Traditional B2B segmentation relied on firmographics, industry, and job title. It assumed that a 'head of data at a Series C company' was a reliable persona. But that assumption no longer holds. Buyers are not just defined by who they are – they are defined by how they buy, who they trust, what their current context is, and how urgently they need a solution.

Segmentation today is self-directed. A CTO might act like an early adopter in one category and a risk-averse skeptic in another. A mid-level manager might carry more buying power in a flat org than a VP in a hierarchical one. Context trumps title. Intent trumps ideal customer profile (ICP). Buyer behavior is dynamic, not fixed – and GTM teams need to build systems that respond in kind.

This is not a rejection of targeting, it's a call for precision over persona, and feedback loops over rigid definitions.

## The math of growth has broken down

When demand fragments, the assumptions behind traditional growth math fall apart. SLG models assume that known leads can be converted through structured sales processes. PLG models assume that usage will reliably translate into monetization. But when the buyer's journey is non-linear, invisible, or intermittent, these systems break down. Conversion becomes unpredictable. Attribution becomes noisy. Optimization becomes guesswork.

The consequence is that even high-performing teams can appear ineffective – because the underlying model no longer fits the market. Efficiency, speed, and coordination still matter. But they must be directed by real-time sensing, not static plans.

## What this all means

Fragmented demand isn't a challenge that can be solved with better targeting or a new marketing technology (martech) stack. It is a structural shift in how markets behave. It renders traditional GTM execution – designed for predictability – increasingly obsolete. Winning teams won't be the ones with the most refined playbooks. They'll be the ones with the best reflexes.

If AI breaks production logic, and the end of cheap capital breaks financing logic, fragmented demand breaks the market logic. The old system is struggling on every front. What remains is to build a new one.

# Conclusion: You can't play the old game on a new board

### The end of static PMF

Individually, each of the shifts we've covered – AI, the end of cheap capital, and the fragmentation of demand – would be enough to warrant a re-evaluation of growth strategy. Together, they represent a full systemic reset. They are not parallel challenges. They are interlocking accelerants. Each one makes the others more disruptive, and more urgent to address.

- AI undermines the logic of scale and efficiency.
- The post-ZIRP financial regime punishes any model that delays profitability.
- Fragmented demand renders traditional GTM execution ineffective and traditional customer insight unreliable.

And underneath them all, the time horizon for PMF itself is collapsing.

PMF was once a milestone. You found it, locked it in, and built your company around it. That model was only viable because markets were relatively stable, competitors couldn't match your feature set overnight, and feedback loops took months to complete. But those constraints are gone. In AI-enabled markets, product, pricing, and user experience (UX) can now evolve in real time. Competitors can replicate surface-level innovations almost instantly, and customer expectations are fragmenting faster than product teams can model them.

The result is that PMF is no longer a fixed point, it's a moving target – and increasingly, a looping function. What fits today may not fit tomorrow, not because the market has shifted, but because the tools available to your competitors have allowed them to collapse the gap between idea and execution. Fit must be constantly re-earned, and the companies that win will not be those that discover PMF once, but those that treat PMF as a continuous operational discipline.

This breaks the old game. The linear model – build, scale, optimize – assumes stasis. It assumes a stable foundation on which to construct process and scale. But the new terrain doesn't offer that foundation, it shifts too quickly, it demands a different motion – sense, adapt, learn, repeat.

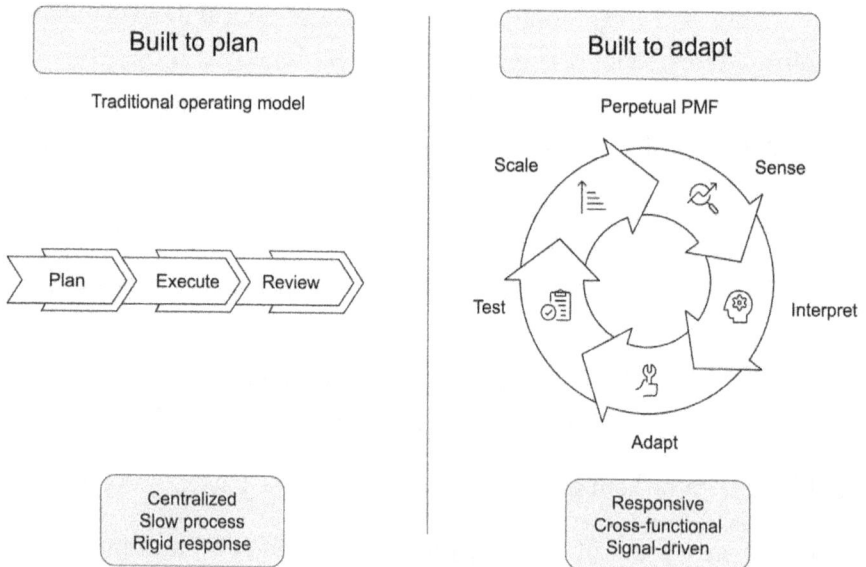

**Figure 4** The traditional model assumes stability; the new model embraces constant change. One was designed for efficiency. The other is designed to evolve.

Most organizations are still structured for the old game. Their planning cycles are too slow, their functions too siloed, their systems too rigid. Even their most well-run playbooks struggle to keep up – not because they're flawed, but because they're fixed.

That's why this book doesn't offer a new playbook, it lays out a new operating model – one built for volatility, designed for responsiveness, and capable of moving at the speed of change. A model that treats mutation as the default state – and growth as the outcome of signal and adaptation, not just scaling.

By now, the accelerants reshaping the terrain should be clear: AI has disrupted the logic of production, capital has become cautious and constrained, and demand has fragmented beyond the reach of traditional channels. These are not isolated shifts. They compound one another.

## Who will be hit hardest?

The systemic reset we've just described – AI-native execution, capital scarcity, and fragmented demand – is not evenly distributed. Some companies are structurally more exposed than others. Their products are easier to replicate. Their markets move faster. Their cost structures depend on assumptions that no longer hold. These companies cannot afford to treat what's coming as a tactical disruption. They need a different operating model.

Others will feel the impact more slowly. Their customer relationships may be stickier, or their products harder to digitize. But proximity to the disruption 'vortex' isn't just about industry. It's about how much of your value relies on knowledge work, how dependent you are on capital to grow, and how dynamic your market has become. The more those conditions apply, the less time you have.

## The center: Software, SaaS, and digital infrastructure

Software companies sit at the center of the vortex. They sell encoded knowledge work, often to other knowledge workers, and now, AI can produce and replace much of what they build. Most software-as-a-service (SaaS) firms scaled by optimizing funnels and funding growth through venture capital. But their playbooks were designed for predictability – not volatility.

Martech, devtools, analytics platforms, workflow automation tools: these companies are seeing core parts of their offering absorbed into AI-native products or replaced outright. Differentiation erodes. Margins compress. GTM costs rise as channels fragment. What worked at US$5M annual recurring revenue (ARR) no longer works at US$50M, and the next stage of growth can't be brute-forced through additional headcount or spend.

These companies are not just facing competition. They're facing a breakdown in the economic logic that underpinned their scale. Their challenge isn't to execute better, it's to operate differently.

## Under pressure: Professional services and expert networks

Law firms, consultancies, design agencies, and financial advisors don't rely on capital in the same way, but they still face a fundamental problem: they sell expertise by the hour, and AI is rapidly compressing the time and cost of delivering that expertise.

The initial impact is bottom-up. Junior associates and analysts are most at risk, as AI begins to handle first-draft analysis, document prep, and synthesis. But over time, the entire model begins to shift. The pyramid flattens. Pricing power weakens. Even if clients still trust senior experts, they no longer want to pay for the labor underneath them.

What protects these firms – for now – is their reputation, client loyalty, and regulatory entrenchment. But none of those are permanent. As AI-native service firms emerge, offering the same outputs with fewer layers and faster delivery, the traditional model will come under sustained pressure.

## Caught in transition: Media, education, and recruitment

Some industries act as intermediaries between knowledge and the customer – packaging content, matching people to opportunities, or providing scalable instruction. These include media, education, and recruitment. All are being reshaped.

In media, AI-generated content floods the web. Readers can get summaries, analyses, and synthetic news faster and cheaper. Legacy publishers, already struggling with revenue models, now compete with infinite supply. The same is beginning to unfold in TV and streaming, where generative tools can produce scripts, visuals, and even entire short-form formats at near-zero cost. Brand and trust are still moats, but without constant attention and work, they are getting shallower by the day.

Education platforms face AI tutors that adapt in real time, generate personalized exercises, and assess performance. The value of passive content delivery declines. What matters is learning design and outcomes – a way of thinking many educational incumbents aren't structured to own.

Recruitment is increasingly automated: CVs scored by models, interviews pre-screened by bots, assessments dynamically generated. The firms built around human filters now compete with systems that offer faster matches and less friction.

The underlying pattern is the same. When the cost of distribution drops and the barrier to entry collapses, intermediaries either evolve or get bypassed.

## More insulated, but not immune: Physical goods and infrastructure

Manufacturers, logistics providers, utilities, and consumer-packaged-goods (CPG) firms are not selling software or advice. They sell

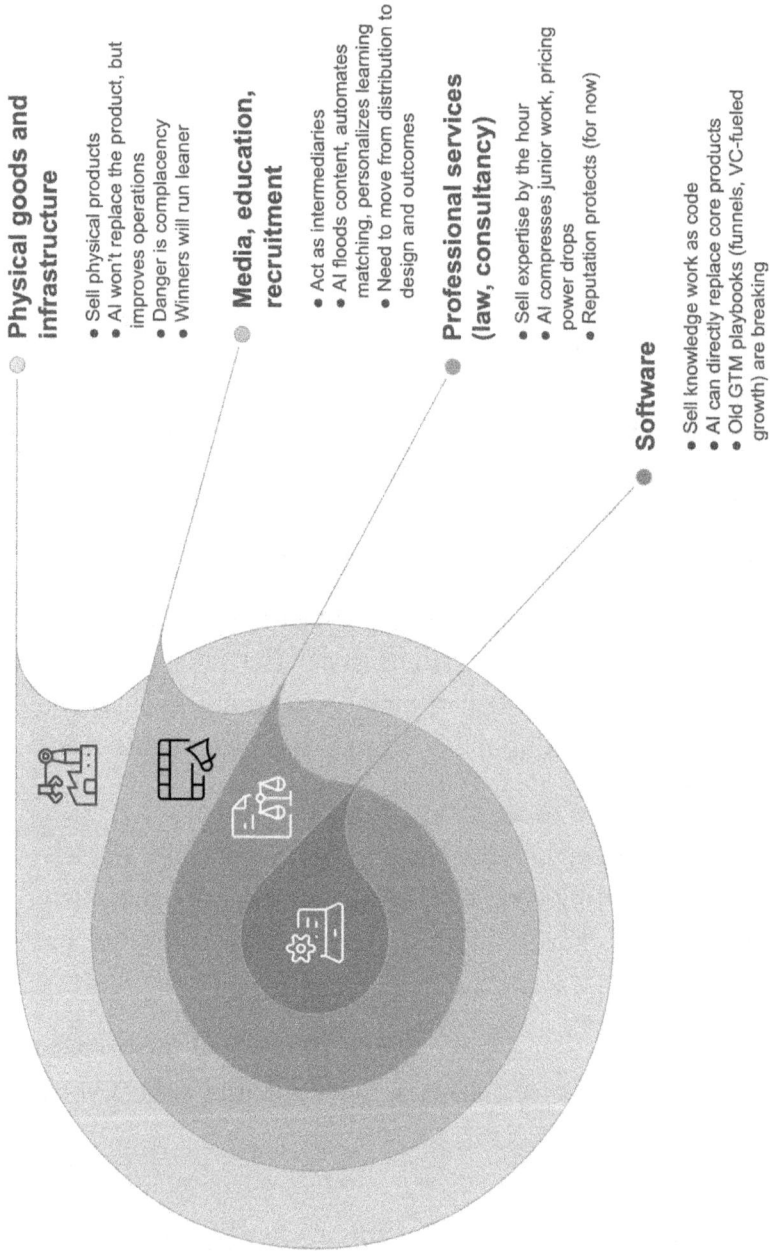

**Physical goods and infrastructure**
- Sell physical products
- AI won't replace the product, but improves operations
- Danger is complacency
- Winners will run leaner

**Media, education, recruitment**
- Act as intermediaries
- AI floods content, automates matching, personalizes learning
- Need to move from distribution to design and outcomes

**Professional services (law, consultancy)**
- Sell expertise by the hour
- AI compresses junior work, pricing power drops
- Reputation protects (for now)

**Software**
- Sell knowledge work as code
- AI can directly replace core products
- Old GTM playbooks (funnels, VC-fueled growth) are breaking

**Figure 5** AI disruption vortex. How close are you to the vortex? Every business faces the same structural shifts – but not on the same timeline. The closer you are to the vortex, the less time you have to adapt.

things – physical, regulated, and often capital-intensive. That gives them a buffer. AI won't replace a tire, a shipping container, or a solar array.

But the buffer is not a moat. AI is already optimizing maintenance schedules, routing logistics, personalizing marketing, and reducing waste. These firms may not face product disruption, but they face execution disruption, and the winners will be those who rewire fastest.

The risk here is complacency. Because the disruption doesn't arrive at the product level, it's easier to ignore. But over time, firms that operate more responsively – on signal – will run leaner, adapt faster, and capture more margin. The shift will be subtle, then sudden.

## Where you sit determines how fast you must move

This book is relevant to every company that wants to grow in today's environment. But not every company has the same time horizon. If you're at the center of the vortex, you are already being disrupted – even if your dashboards haven't caught up. You can't afford to wait for perfect information or incremental change. You need to redesign how you work now.

If you're further from the center, you still face the same structural shifts – just with more time and more optionality. That's both an opportunity and a trap. Because the longer you delay adaptation, the harder it becomes to catch up. Either way, the logic of growth has changed.

In the next chapter, we'll go deeper into why so many companies are struggling to adapt – not because they've chosen the wrong tactics, but because their operating playbooks no longer fit the environment they're in. The rest of the book is about how to respond – not with a new playbook, but with a new operating model built for speed, signal, and sustained adaptability.

# 2

# The broken playbooks

Go-to-market (GTM) models are supposed to be execution strategies. At their best, they are ways of organizing teams, workflows, and pricing around a clear theory of how to reach and convert customers. But over the past decade, two such strategies – Sales-Led Growth (SLG) and Product-Led Growth (PLG) – have evolved into something much more rigid. They became identities, philosophies, almost religious belief systems.

You weren't just using a sales-led or product-led motion. You *were* a sales-led or product-led company. That label shaped how you hired, how you built, how you marketed, how you measured success. Entire organizational architectures were constructed around a single dominant growth model – assuming that the path to scale was fixed, repeatable, and defensible.

In many ways, it worked. SLG allowed companies to navigate complexity and sell high-value products through human-driven persuasion. PLG enabled rapid expansion through user-driven adoption and efficient viral loops. Each model defined a generation of category leaders. But the very thing that made them successful – their clarity and consistency – has become the source of their fragility.

The mistake wasn't in using SLG or PLG, it was in *treating them as static blueprints rather than dynamic tools*. Instead of evolving their GTM approach as conditions changed, most companies committed fully to one model and scaled it as far as possible. But in a world where markets shift weekly, capital is constrained, and product-market fit (PMF) is a moving target, that level of rigidity is a liability.

SLG and PLG are not inherently broken. They were built for specific conditions that no longer exist. When misapplied or overstretched, they lead companies into structural traps: SLG into bloat and inertia, PLG into commoditization and stalled monetization. Hybrid models, far from solving the problem, often compound it by introducing complexity without clarity.

This chapter isn't an attack on these models, it's a postmortem. A respectful but clear-eyed look at how and why these growth engines stall – and what that tells us about the kind of system we need now. Because if SLG and PLG were the operating models of the last era, we will need something fundamentally more flexible for the next.

Let's begin with SLG: the motion that defined enterprise software – and now risks defining its stagnation.

## Section 1: The SLG trap – when the operating model hardens

### Why SLG worked (then)

SLG was never a bad idea. For most of the last two decades, it was the most reliable way to scale a technology company, particularly in complex or risk-averse markets. SLG succeeded because it matched the dominant buyer behavior of the time. Enterprise buyers needed to be educated, reassured, and de-risked. Procurement cycles were formal, multi-stage processes. Technology purchasing was expensive, high-stakes, and career-defining for the executives making the decisions. In that environment, human-led enterprise sales was not just useful – it was essential.

The economics of SLG reflected this complexity. High customer acquisition costs (CAC) were justified because each deal carried a correspondingly high average selling price (ASP) and multi-year contract value. Winning a new customer meant securing a durable, defensible revenue stream. The upfront investment in sales was offset by predictable cash flows and stable expansion opportunities.

Importantly, SLG worked in a world where markets moved slowly, and new competitors emerged gradually. Feature differentiation, once established, could last for years. Procurement inertia favored incumbents. The result was that once a company secured its foothold through SLG, it could build moats around its customer base that were difficult to erode. The initial cost and complexity of the model were acceptable trade-offs for the stability and scalability it unlocked.

In that world, organizing a company entirely around an SLG motion made strategic sense. Hiring was structured around sales coverage. Product roadmaps prioritized the needs of high-value accounts. Marketing acted in service of sales enablement. Revenue predictability outweighed experimentation. Efficiency was measured by how tightly GTM and product could align to the enterprise sales cycle.

For a long time, this alignment produced category leaders, it was optimized for the conditions in which it evolved. But those conditions no longer exist – and the very structures that once made SLG companies strong now make them vulnerable.

## How SLG hardens into a trap

The problem with SLG is not in its logic, but in its tendency to calcify. What begins as a smart GTM decision often becomes an inflexible organizational identity. Over time, the company's structure, incentives, and operational rhythms orient so completely around the SLG motion that adaptation becomes nearly impossible.

The cycle is predictable. High CAC forces companies to maintain high ASPs to sustain margins. But high ASPs inevitably invite heavy customization demands. Enterprise buyers expect products to mold to their unique workflows and requirements – because at those price points, flexibility is table stakes. To land and retain large accounts, companies agree to build custom features, integrations, and support structures tailored to individual customers.

Customization, in turn, drives product bloat. The clean, focused roadmap that existed in the early days gets increasingly distorted by the need to satisfy bespoke enterprise requirements. Engineering teams spend more time maintaining niche features than building new capabilities. Product managers prioritize existing customer demands over market exploration. Innovation slows, not because leadership lacks ambition, but because the system itself rewards incrementalism and punishes disruption.

As the product becomes heavier, execution slows across the board. Every new feature carries higher risk. Every architecture change requires negotiation with major accounts. Every pricing adjustment threatens carefully balanced multi-year deals. Meanwhile, the GTM organization becomes optimized not for sensing new opportunities, but for defending existing ones. Sales leadership focuses on expanding within installed bases. Marketing becomes lead generation for a fixed ideal customer profile. Strategy meetings become exercises in forecast protection, not opportunity creation.

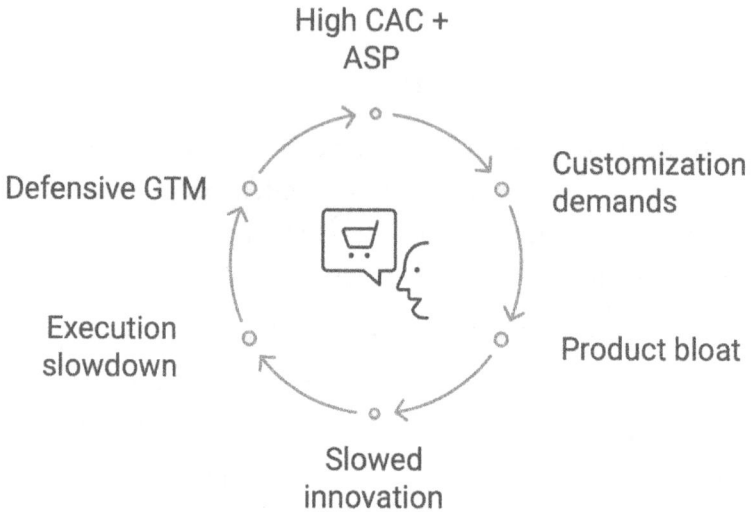

**Figure 6** The SLG trap. 'It's a trap!' said no CRO ever. But they should have seen this coming, just like Ackbar.

The most dangerous aspect of the SLG trap is that it doesn't feel like failure – until it's too late. Revenue may continue growing, but at a steadily decelerating rate. CAC may creep upward, but it is rationalized as necessary to 'go upmarket' or 'maintain strategic accounts.' Product launches become less frequent, less differentiated, but this is justified internally as 'focusing on customer success and experience.'

By the time the external market moves decisively – when competitors undercut on price, when new entrants attack from below, when customers demand new capabilities – the company's operating model is too rigid to respond at the necessary speed. The SLG operating system, once a source of competitive advantage, becomes an anchor.

## The compounding dynamics of the SLG trap

Once the structural dynamics of SLG begin to harden, the problems rarely stay isolated – they compound.

High CAC locks companies into high ASP pricing strategies. But as market conditions evolve – competition increases, budgets tighten, procurement becomes more value-conscious – maintaining those high ASPs becomes harder. Discounting creeps in, renewal negotiations become more adversarial, and expansion slows.

Yet the GTM cost base – built to support a high-touch sales motion – remains fixed or even grows. Sales organizations are difficult to shrink without risking top-line revenue. Enterprise customer support expectations, once promised, are expensive to unwind.

Meanwhile, product complexity increases the cost of innovation. Every adjustment carries downstream risks across a fragile and interdependent codebase. Even when leadership recognizes the need for change – a pivot to a usage-based model, a shift toward a lower-cost offering, a reorientation around a new buyer persona – the operational reality of executing that change is daunting. Product development timelines are longer. Customer success teams resist feature retirements. Sales teams fear introducing new products that could cannibalize or confuse existing accounts.

This can also become a platform trap. As SLG companies try to manage bespoke enterprise demands, they often evolve into sprawling platforms – configurable, flexible, and deeply entangled. But instead of serving business users directly, they end up catering to IT departments, system integrators, and solution architects. The customer – the end user actually trying to get something done – gets further from the product. Worse, this abstraction creates misaligned incentives. Integrators benefit from complexity. End users want speed. In a world of disposable apps and AI-generated interfaces, this gap is a dangerous one – because end users will soon be able to design and deploy their own apps without the need for external product at all.

This creates a ratchet effect. Every quarter, the company's options narrow. Incremental optimizations – hiring more reps, adding professional services, expanding partner ecosystems – can buy time, but they do not solve the underlying strategic rigidity: margins compress; CAC continues to rise; revenue growth slows despite increasing spend; and because the structures of the company are optimized for a particular sales motion, not for sensing and responding to market shifts, early warning signs are often misinterpreted as tactical execution failures rather than symptoms of strategic obsolescence.

Leadership meetings focus on hiring plans, pipeline coverage, and quarterly forecasts. Less time is spent questioning whether the GTM motion itself still fits the market terrain. Even when individuals sense that the system is under strain, institutional inertia – and fear of destabilizing existing revenue streams – prevents meaningful course correction.

The result is predictable: a slow, grinding loss of agility that only becomes fully visible once growth stalls and churn accelerates. At that point, recovery is possible but extraordinarily difficult. It requires not just adjusting tactics, but dismantling and rebuilding the operating system itself – something few organizations are prepared to do under pressure.

The SLG trap is not a sudden failure, it is a long, gradual tightening of constraints, each logical in isolation, but collectively fatal in a world where the speed of market mutation has accelerated beyond an organization's ability to adapt.

## Case study: Snowflake – when success locks you in

At its peak, Snowflake seemed invincible, its combination of technical innovation, enterprise-grade reliability, and a textbook SLG execution playbook made it the dominant force in the cloud data warehousing market. From its 2020 IPO through fiscal 2023, Snowflake posted extraordinary numbers: product revenue grew 70% year-over-year, driven largely by aggressive expansion inside Fortune 500 accounts.[1]

Snowflake's model was pure SLG at scale:

- Large, expensive outbound sales teams targeting enterprise buyers.
- High ASPs supported by complex, multi-year contracts.
- Deep customization and integrations to meet the specific demands of large customers.
- A strong emphasis on land-and-expand strategies, where initial deals were expanded over time through heavy relationship management.

This playbook worked – until it didn't.

---

[1] Snowflake Inc., 'Snowflake Reports Financial Results for the Fourth Quarter and Full Year of Fiscal 2023,' *Snowflake Newsroom*, March 1, 2023, www.snowflake.com/en/news/press-releases/snowflake-reports-financial-results-for-the-fourth-quarter-and-full-year-of-fiscal-2023/

## *The warning signs appear*

Starting in fiscal 2024, Snowflake's revenue growth began to slow – first to 38% year-over-year, then down to 29% by Q3 of fiscal 2025.[2] While 29% growth would be enviable for many companies, for a business valued on expectations of perpetual hypergrowth, it signaled a major inflection point.

The external pressures were clear:

- **Increased competition** from AWS Redshift, Google BigQuery, Databricks, and Microsoft Azure Synapse, all of which began bundling comparable data solutions deeper into their broader cloud ecosystems.
- **Pricing pressure** as customers compared Snowflake's complex usage-based pricing models against more integrated, predictable alternatives.
- **Feature parity** as competitors accelerated their development roadmaps, collapsing the technical gap Snowflake once held.

But Snowflake's real challenge was not competition, it was its own internal operating system – the rigidity of a full-scale SLG model that made strategic adaptation extremely difficult.

## *The SLG trap in action*

Snowflake's commitment to its original GTM motion had hardwired certain realities into its business:

1. **High-cost structure**
   - Maintaining massive enterprise sales teams meant CAC remained structurally high, even as revenue growth slowed.

---

[2] Snowflake Inc., 'Quarterly Results.' *Investor Relations – Snowflake*, accessed June 29, 2025, https://investors.snowflake.com/financials/quarterly-results/default.aspx

       o  Outbound sales motion reinforced the need for complex, expensive engagements rather than simpler, product-led expansions.

2. **Product complexity**
   o Customization for large accounts had increased the surface area of the product substantially.
   o Engineering teams spent increasing cycles maintaining, rather than innovating, as the product accumulated feature debt.

3. **Pricing rigidity**
   o Complex, consumption-based pricing models, while initially attractive, became friction points for customers seeking predictability.
   o Simplifying pricing without alienating existing customers or sacrificing margin became politically and operationally difficult.

4. **Cultural inertia**
   o The entire organization – from Sales to Product to Finance – was optimized for the high-touch, large-deal SLG model.
   o Pivoting to a lower-cost, mid-market, or usage-led strategy would have required fundamental shifts in hiring, training, product management, and financial planning.

These compounding factors meant that even when external market conditions shifted, Snowflake's most viable path – doubling down on enterprise sales – was also the path that increased fragility.

## The strategic dilemma

Snowflake faced a strategic paradox common to maturing SLG companies:

- **Maintain the existing model**, betting that expansion within large accounts and upselling new services would offset slowing new logo growth, while accepting margin pressure and slowing operating leverage.

- **Attempt a pivot** toward lower-cost, more flexible GTM motions that could unlock broader market segments – but at the risk of destabilizing revenue forecasts, upsetting large customers, and undermining internal coherence.

Predictably, Snowflake chose the former. In fiscal 2025, the company announced continued investment in enterprise sales expansion rather than significant structural change. It was a rational decision given the immediate pressures of public market expectations, but it further locked the company into the SLG trap. Growth continued to decelerate, margins compressed, investor sentiment – once exuberant – began to cool.

What made this even more stark was the contrast with Databricks, which capitalized early on the GenAI wave. While Snowflake was doubling down on its role as a high-performance data warehouse for enterprise IT, Databricks positioned itself as the engine room for AI-native development – flexible, developer-oriented, and integrated with emerging machine-learning workflows. As interest in agentic AI systems accelerated, customers increasingly saw Snowflake as a backend workhorse. It was infrastructure – reliable, fast, but ultimately peripheral to where innovation was happening.

This wasn't just a perception issue. In direct conversations with Snowflake's GTM team as recently as April 2024, it was clear that the path of least resistance – and highest commission – was to sell Snowflake as the data layer beneath existing product stacks. There was little emphasis on generative AI, little positioning around emergent use cases, and few signals that the company was preparing to lead rather than follow. That same month, Frank Slootman announced his resignation as CEO. The timing was telling.

Slootman had taken the company to the stratosphere by executing SLG with discipline and precision, but also locked Snowflake into revenue streams that were comfortable and linear – streams that left little room for sensing or responding to the market's next inflection point. In a world shifting toward composable systems, continuous adaptation, and GenAI-native architecture, that strategic conservatism became a liability.

## The lesson from Snowflake

Snowflake's story is not a case of poor execution, it is a case of structural rigidity. SLG delivered extraordinary growth in an environment that rewarded scale and complexity. But as the market shifted toward integration, simplicity, and cost transparency, Snowflake's operating model left it poorly positioned to adapt at the necessary speed.

The real failure was not in choosing SLG early on – it was in allowing SLG to become the company's operating identity, rather than treating it as a tactical choice that could evolve over time.

Snowflake remains a formidable company. But its experience offers a stark warning: in volatile markets, success built on a static model becomes a trap. Without the ability to unbundle growth strategy from organizational structure, even the best companies can find themselves locked into motions that no longer fit the terrain.

## Why SLG companies struggle to see it coming

The structural fragility of SLG often goes unrecognized until it is too late – not because leadership is negligent, but because the system masks its own decline.

When growth slows, the symptoms resemble execution problems, not strategy problems. Deals take longer to close, so the solution is to hire more account executives. Churn rises, so the response is to expand customer success teams. Pricing pressure emerges, so the answer is deeper discounting or bespoke packaging. Each tactic addresses the immediate pain point without questioning whether the underlying GTM model still fits the market.

This defensive posture compounds over time. Leadership focuses on optimizing an increasingly brittle system, believing that with enough operational rigor, the old model will regain traction. Sales incentives, marketing spend, customer success coverage – everything is adjusted around the margins. What is rarely addressed is the possibility that the operating assumptions themselves – high ASPs, heavy customization, long-cycle sales motions – are no longer aligned with how customers want to buy.

By the time the diagnosis shifts from execution failure to strategic misalignment, the company's options are limited. Retrenching the sales-team risks immediate revenue loss. Simplifying the product risks alienating key accounts. Shifting GTM structure risks cultural destabilization. Rationally, leadership often chooses to defend the status quo, even as its structural viability erodes.

This is the real cost of letting a GTM motion ossify into an organizational identity. It traps companies not just operationally, but cognitively. The system becomes incapable of seeing that the terrain has shifted – and by the time reality forces recognition, escape is extraordinarily difficult.

## Section 2: The PLG trap – when low-cost growth becomes an expensive liability

### PLG's original promise and its hidden fragility

PLG reshaped the software-as-a-service (SaaS) landscape by making user adoption frictionless. Instead of relying on expensive, human-driven sales processes, PLG companies let the product sell itself: lower the barriers to entry, allow users to experience value directly, and convert that engagement into revenue over time. In theory, PLG offered a powerful formula – low CAC, rapid scale, and a natural, organic expansion motion that could compound without the heavy overhead of traditional sales organizations.

In practice, it worked. Some of the most iconic technology companies of the past decade – Dropbox, Atlassian, Slack – achieved extraordinary early growth by mastering the PLG motion. They proved that products could drive adoption directly, that network effects could be built from the bottom up, and that virality could replace outbound marketing as the engine of expansion.

But embedded within PLG's success story was a structural weakness: its dependence on external conditions that would not persist. PLG thrived in an environment where digital channels were underutilized, acquisition costs were low, and market categories were immature. As those conditions changed – saturation of acquisition channels, rising customer expectations, commoditization of core features – the very advantages that made PLG so compelling began to erode.

The risk with PLG is not in the motion itself. Again, it's in *mistaking a stage or market-specific tactic for a complete and permanent operating system.* Many companies scaled initial adoption beautifully, but failed to evolve their models as the environment or market shifted. They assumed that the mechanisms which fueled their early growth would continue to operate at scale. When they didn't, the fragility of PLG at maturity became apparent – and often, the drawbacks irreversible.

## Why PLG worked (then)

PLG emerged as a rational, strategic response to a specific set of market conditions.

First, digital distribution channels offered unprecedented reach at minimal cost. Search engine optimization (SEO), app stores, social sharing, and content-driven inbound marketing created efficient pathways to attract users without relying on human touchpoints. A well-designed onboarding experience, a freemium model, and a clear time-to-value could generate viral growth loops that were both effective and cheap.

Second, user expectations aligned with product simplicity. In the early 2010s, users were actively seeking lightweight, accessible tools that could solve discrete problems without the complexity of enterprise software. Products that emphasized ease of use, quick deployment, and immediate value creation had a natural advantage over heavier, procurement-driven offerings.

Third, competitive landscapes were less saturated. Being first or early to market with a compelling freemium (pricing strategy where the basic product is provided for free, but then users are charged for additional features) or low-cost product often created natural monopolies or near-monopolies within key usage categories. Network effects reinforced early mover advantages, making it difficult for competitors to displace established PLG players once they had achieved critical mass.

Fourth, freemium dynamics aligned well with market psychology. Offering a free tier lowered friction dramatically, encouraging mass adoption. A meaningful percentage of users could be expected to convert to paid plans as they scaled usage or hit feature limits, creating a self-sustaining funnel that required little incremental cost to maintain.

The result was a set of economics that made PLG look, for a time, unstoppable:

- Low CAC.
- High viral coefficient.
- Predictable self-serve expansion.
- Minimal reliance on expensive, high-touch sales resources.

It is no surprise that many companies built their entire operating models around these assumptions. When acquisition is cheap, product-led onboarding is efficient, and free-to-paid conversion is consistent, PLG looks not just like a growth strategy, but like a fundamental law of business.

But laws, in business, are usually just temporary conditions in disguise.

As markets matured, competition intensified, and acquisition channels became saturated, the conditions that made PLG scalable at low cost began to erode. What once was a superpower increasingly became a constraint – one that many companies found themselves structurally unprepared to escape.

## How PLG hardens into a trap

The early successes of PLG created an operational momentum that was difficult to resist. When user acquisition is cheap, conversion rates are stable, and viral loops are compounding, there is little incentive to re-examine underlying assumptions. Organizational structures, product roadmaps, marketing motions, and leadership philosophies all align around a model that appears to be working.

But as markets evolve, that very alignment becomes rigidity. The model that enabled initial growth starts to introduce hidden liabilities that are difficult to correct at scale.

The first structural pressure comes from rising customer acquisition costs. As more competitors enter a market, digital channels become saturated. Paid search, social advertising, content marketing – tactics that once delivered low-CAC users at scale now face diminishing returns. Organic acquisition slows as search algorithms evolve and as buyer attention fragments across a wider array of platforms and communities. To sustain growth, PLG companies find themselves spending heavily to acquire users who once arrived on their own.

At the same time, pricing power erodes. As freemium becomes the standard across categories, user expectations shift. What was once perceived as premium functionality becomes baseline expectation. Companies are forced to offer more for free just to maintain acquisition velocity. Each addition to the free tier delays the point at which users hit a meaningful paywall, dragging down conversion rates and suppressing ASPs.

These two dynamics create a vicious cycle:

- CAC rises.
- Monetization lags.
- Free users grow faster than paying customers.
- Cost to serve increases without corresponding revenue uplift.

The natural instinct is to try to compensate through feature expansion – building more functionality, offering more integrations, creating

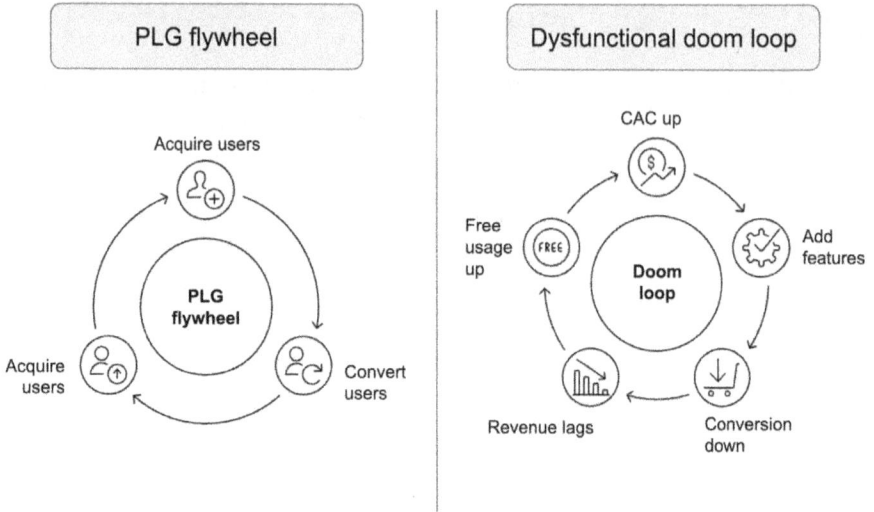

**Figure 7** These traps just keep piling up, huh? This one's a doom loop, sounds like a Marvel character. Frankly, this one is far scarier.

premium tiers. But every new feature adds complexity: onboarding becomes harder, support costs rise, and the product drifts away from the simplicity that originally fueled viral adoption.

## The organizational consequences of stalled PLG

As this pressure mounts, PLG companies face a critical choice: change their GTM system, or double down on optimizing the existing model.

Often, they choose the latter – not because leadership is blind, but because the internal structures, culture, and investor expectations are all tuned to PLG dynamics. Adding a sales motion feels like a betrayal of the founding philosophy. Rethinking the pricing model risks alienating the free user base that was once celebrated as a sign of success. Investing in segmentation or account-based strategies feels antithetical to the core idea of frictionless, self-serve growth.

This cultural rigidity mirrors the structural rigidity seen in mature SLG companies, but with different surface symptoms. Where SLG companies defend high ASPs and enterprise feature bloat, PLG companies defend free acquisition and simplicity – even when those no longer produce the intended outcomes.

Without intervention, the PLG trap compounds:

- Marketing spend rises faster than revenue.
- Engineering teams are stretched thin maintaining both free and paid tiers.
- Revenue teams struggle to find leverage points for expansion.
- Free user bases grow impressive in size but hollow in monetizable value.

By the time leadership recognizes that the model is no longer working, the path to reinvention – adding enterprise sales, repositioning the brand, restructuring pricing – requires a level of disruption that feels existential. Many companies hesitate. They iterate around the edges. They add onboarding flows, tweak pricing tiers, invest in brand. But without a fundamental reworking of the GTM engine, the outcome is inevitable: growth stalls, margins compress, and strategic options narrow.

PLG, like SLG, is not inherently flawed, it is situational. When treated as a permanent operating model rather than a tactical stage, it leads companies into traps from which they are structurally ill-prepared to escape.

## Case study: Twilio – the limits of early PLG success

Twilio is often cited as a quintessential PLG success story. Founded in 2008, it pioneered an API-driven approach to communications infrastructure, allowing developers to easily embed voice, messaging, and authentication features into their applications. Its core motion was classic PLG: low-friction adoption, pay-as-you-go pricing, developer-first onboarding, and rapid viral spread through technical communities.

For years, this model delivered extraordinary growth. Twilio captured mindshare among startups and engineering teams globally. Its revenue scaled rapidly without the heavy investment in traditional enterprise sales forces seen in its contemporaries. Its self-serve model allowed developers to start using the product without procurement cycles or sales engagement, creating organic adoption paths that looked, for a time, almost infinitely scalable.

But as Twilio matured, the limits of its PLG-driven model began to emerge. Not because the company executed poorly, but because the underlying market dynamics shifted – and the operating system built for early-stage adoption struggled to adapt to late-stage complexity.

## The early strength of Twilio's PLG motion

In its formative years, Twilio benefited from several reinforcing advantages:

- **Low initial CAC**: Developer adoption spread through word-of-mouth, conferences, and content without requiring heavy marketing spend.
- **High initial stickiness**: Once integrated into an application, communication APIs were costly and inconvenient to swap out, creating strong early retention.
- **Simple, transparent pricing**: Developers could pay only for what they used, aligning incentives perfectly for early adoption.
- **Expansion via usage growth**: As customer applications scaled, so did Twilio's billing, creating a natural expansion motion without sales intervention.

For a while, this model seemed self-reinforcing. More users led to more integrations, which led to more usage, which led to more revenue – all without the traditional costs and frictions associated with enterprise GTM strategies.

## The market matures – and friction grows

However, as Twilio scaled beyond its initial user base, three structural pressures began to build:

1. **Rising CAC across digital channels**
   o The once-underpriced digital acquisition channels –
     search, paid social, developer community sponsorships –
     became more crowded and expensive.
   o Organic developer adoption slowed as new competitors
     flooded the market with comparable offerings and
     aggressive incentives.
2. **Enterprise buyer behavior shifted**
   o As Twilio's customer base evolved from startups to large
     enterprises, procurement processes reasserted themselves.
   o Enterprise IT departments demanded integration assur-
     ances, security certifications, custom SLAs, and pricing
     negotiations that could not be handled via self-serve
     motions alone.
3. **Pricing complexity and friction increased**
   o Twilio's consumption-based model, while attractive to
     developers, created billing unpredictability for larger
     accounts.
   o Enterprise buyers, particularly CFOs, grew wary of
     usage-based spend volatility, seeking fixed contracts and
     discount structures that strained Twilio's original model.

In short, the world that Twilio's PLG motion was built for changed. The
company now had to serve two radically different customer bases: the
independent developer looking for simple, pay-as-you-go access, and
the enterprise IT department seeking predictability, service levels, and
commercial negotiation.

The original PLG engine, built for one environment, was not naturally
suited to the next.

## *The organizational tensions of scaling beyond PLG*

To address these shifts, Twilio began to layer in a traditional enterprise
sales force. But this transition was far from smooth.

- **CAC rose sharply**: Hiring and lead-times for training enterprise reps added significant costs to the GTM structure.
- **Sales and product tensions grew**: Enterprise sales teams pushed for customizations, multi-product bundling, and complex pricing – moves that often conflicted with Twilio's product simplicity ethos.
- **Brand perception lagged**: Twilio was still widely perceived as a 'developer tool,' making it harder to position itself credibly against more established enterprise software vendors.
- **Self-serve adoption flattened**: As free and low-cost entry points became saturated and marginal acquisition costs rose, Twilio's original growth loops slowed.

The result was not a sudden failure, but a slow erosion of operating leverage. Revenue continued to grow, but margins compressed, operating costs climbed, and the distance between top-line success and bottom-line profitability widened.

Twilio's problems were compounded by its difficulty integrating acquisitions like Segment and SendGrid into a coherent enterprise story. While each product held promise, the company struggled to unify them into a portfolio that felt strategic rather than piecemeal. Segment, in particular, became a drag on growth, not because of market failure, but because Twilio lacked the operating model to orchestrate multi-product value creation. The company was built to scale individual application programming interfaces (APIs), not bundle them into enterprise platforms, and so, the PLG mindset – brilliant at early traction – left Twilio ill-equipped to tell a unified enterprise story.

By early 2023, the strain was visible. Twilio announced layoffs impacting 17% of its workforce, citing the need to cut costs and focus on profitable growth.[3] Leadership publicly acknowledged the

---

[3] Jeff Lawson, 'Restructuring Twilio, and Reducing the Size of Our Team,' *Twilio Blog*, February 13, 2023, www.twilio.com/en-us/blog/company/news/restructuring-twilio

need to simplify operations and better align to an enterprise-driven future. But these moves, while necessary, were reactive rather than strategic – symptoms of a company grappling with the realization that its founding motion was no longer sufficient.

## The lesson from Twilio

Twilio's trajectory is not an indictment of PLG. Rather, it is a demonstration of PLG's situational limits. A product-led motion can drive extraordinary early-stage growth, particularly when market conditions align. But if the company does not change its operating model to match the demands of later-stage buyers, the very strengths that enabled early success become friction points.

The challenge is not technical, it is organizational. Building and scaling an enterprise sales force, repositioning brand narratives, adjusting pricing models, and aligning cross-functional incentives around new buyer needs requires transformation at every level: product, marketing, sales, finance, leadership.

That transition is hard – especially when the founding mythology, the early growth metrics, and the internal culture are all tied to the success of the original PLG engine.

Twilio remains a substantial company. Its APIs still power critical infrastructure across industries. But its struggles to transition from a pure PLG model to a hybrid GTM motion offer a clear warning: growth models are not static assets. They are bets on specific environmental conditions. When those conditions change, companies must be willing to change their models – or risk being trapped by them.

### Why PLG companies struggle to see it coming

PLG companies rarely recognize the structural limits of their model until they are well into the stall.

In the early phases, growth is both fast and efficient. CAC is low, adoption is organic, and user metrics climb consistently. But these signals can be misleading. A growing free user base may conceal flatlining monetization. Viral loops may look healthy even as expansion revenue slows. The surface metrics tell a success story, while the economic core quietly deteriorates.

As pressure builds, companies tend to misdiagnose the problem. Slowing paid conversions are blamed on onboarding friction. Declining ASPs trigger calls for new pricing tiers. Churn among free users is written off as natural attrition. Each response is tactical – more content, more features, more nudges – none of which address the underlying issue: the model has stopped working at scale.

Even when the warning signs are clear, strategic adaptation is difficult. Adding a sales motion feels culturally antithetical. Repositioning the product for higher-paying segments risks alienating the very community that drove early growth. Investors who bought into the PLG narrative may resist changes that suggest the engine is faltering.

As with SLG, the greatest risk isn't in the model – it's in treating the model as doctrine. When a GTM strategy becomes a belief system, the company loses its ability to adapt, and in a fast-moving market, that inability spells trouble.

## Conclusion: Fixed growth models in a fluid market

The breakdown of SLG and PLG is not random, it is the result of structural misalignment with a market environment that has changed faster than most companies have been willing – or able – to adapt to.

As we saw in Chapter 1, three forces are converging to rewrite the rules of growth:

1. **AI is collapsing the cost and time to build**, making differentiation fragile and compressing the product lifecycle.
2. **The post-ZIRP era has made capital expensive and risk tolerance low**, forcing hard tradeoffs between growth and efficiency.
3. **Buyer behavior is fragmenting**, diffusing demand across channels, personas, and ecosystems that traditional GTM structures can't easily navigate.

Together, these forces have transformed PMF from a strategic milestone into a continuous operational challenge. PMF is no longer something you find once and scale around. It's something you have to re-earn – over and over again – as markets shift, competitors mutate, and customer expectations evolve in real time.

SLG and PLG were not built for this world. They were designed for environments where fit was stable, scale brought efficiency, and demand was coherent. When those conditions held, they produced enormous value. But when the terrain changed, their rigidity became a liability. GTM motions that were once assets hardened into identities – fixed models trying to operate in a fluid market.

The natural response has been to try to combine them. To bolt PLG and SLG together into hybrid motions that preserve the best of both. But this rarely works. It introduces cost, confusion, and conflict – without resolving the deeper issue. Hybrid is not inherently wrong. It's just not enough. Because it still treats GTM as a static structure, rather than a dynamic system.

What we need now is a new operating model: one that optimizes not for repeatability, but for adaptability.

# 3

# The Market-Led Growth operating system

## From playbooks to operating systems

The previous chapter ended with a blunt truth: in today's volatile markets, fixed growth models are a liability. Whether Sales-Led, Product-Led, or some hybrid of the two, existing growth models were built for a world of stable buyer behavior and long product cycles. That world no longer exists.

What comes next is not a better playbook, it's a fundamentally different operating model. One built for constant adjustment. One that treats product-market fit (PMF) not as a target, but as a motion – a continuous process of realignment between what you offer and what the market demands.

This is the age of *Perpetual PMF*. Navigating it requires a new kind of company: faster, more decentralized, more reflexive. That's what Market-Led Growth (MLG) makes possible. MLG is not a channel strategy, it is not a department's philosophy, it is a full-stack operating system for companies that intend to stay relevant as conditions change.

What's critical to understand is that this system already exists. MLG is not speculative, it has emerged, piece by piece, in the most adaptive and strategically resilient companies of the last decade. The only thing missing has been a name. But before we lay out the full structure of the MLG model, it's worth asking: what does it actually look like in the real world? You don't need to imagine it. You just need to look closely at Amazon and Microsoft.

Neither company uses the term 'Market-Led Growth.' But both operate with the reflexes and structures that define it. They don't just respond to market shifts. They are built to respond – to act on early signal, decentralize execution, adapt go-to-market (GTM) architecture, and deploy capital fluidly. These aren't one-off decisions. They're system-level capabilities.

And while neither company runs a perfect or complete MLG model, they offer some early proof that this way of operating is not hypothetical. It's already working.

## Amazon: Systemic speed and signal-led execution

Amazon's clearest MLG-aligned decision was its early move into cloud computing. AWS wasn't born from a top-down corporate strategy – it emerged from *internal signal*. What began as a set of internal tools to support Amazon's retail infrastructure was spun out into a commercial offering – but critically, it was treated as a standalone business from the outset.

AWS had its own leadership, its own profit and loss (P&L), and its own product roadmap. It was insulated from the demands of Amazon's core commerce engine. Jeff Bezos committed to it publicly,[1] even as many inside and outside the company questioned its relevance. That commitment allowed AWS to grow patiently, then explosively – eventually becoming Amazon's most profitable and strategically important unit. Without that early separation, AWS would likely have been deprioritized, redirected, or absorbed too soon.

But the real story isn't AWS, it's *how* Amazon made it happen. Internally, Amazon is structured for reflex. Its 'two-pizza teams' are small, cross-functional, and autonomous. They own a specific problem space

---

[1] www.acquired.fm/episodes/amazon-web-services

end-to-end. They don't need central approval to launch something new – or to kill it when it's not working. Kindle, Alexa, Prime – even the 'other products you might like' bar – weren't strategic bets handed down from HQ. They were experiments – run close to the signal, iterated rapidly, and only scaled once traction was proven.

Leadership doesn't micromanage these teams. It creates the conditions for movement: clear constraints, shared metrics, strong defaults – and then gets out of the way. Capital allocation follows suit. Amazon doesn't fund teams based on status or tenure. It funds based on traction. Early wins attract more resources. Projects that stall get wound down without drama. The whole system is designed to follow momentum – not memory. This is what MLG looks like at scale: execution at the edge, strategy that emerges from signal, and an organization that adapts faster than its environment.

## Microsoft: Reinventing at the pace of market mutation

Microsoft's transformation under Satya Nadella is a case study in structural reinvention. The company went from defending entrenched enterprise licenses to becoming one of the most adaptable – and strategically aggressive – platform businesses in tech.

Azure followed a similar trajectory to AWS, but what's more telling is *how* Microsoft adapted its GTM model to match changing buyer behavior. Steve Ballmer empowered Satya Nadella (well before he was CEO) to build the cloud business as a separate unit, with its own mandate, rhythm, and leadership autonomy. Nadella was not operating under the constraints of the traditional Windows or Office franchises. This gave Azure the space to develop a new architecture, a new GTM approach, and a new customer base – without being forced into alignment with Microsoft's legacy incentives or metrics. By the time Nadella became CEO, Azure had already established itself as a credible, independent business line, capable of scaling on its own terms. That autonomy was not incidental, it was foundational. This then led to adaptability beyond Azure:

- **Office 365** transitioned Microsoft from perpetual licenses to software-as-a-service (SaaS) subscriptions. That shift required rethinking product, packaging, and GTM simultaneously – and cannibalizing a legacy cash cow in the process.
- **Teams** became a Trojan horse for both PLG and enterprise collaboration, taking ground from Slack not through pure product superiority, but by moving faster and aligning distribution with emergent user behaviors.
- **Copilot** was launched quickly, even imperfectly, because Microsoft recognized the cost of waiting in a fast-moving AI landscape. Instead of chasing polish, they prioritized *presence* – getting to market, learning live, and iterating fast.

Under Nadella, leadership itself changed posture – from enforcing legacy structures to enabling movement. Microsoft no longer tries to control every variable. It builds flexible execution systems and allows teams to adapt them in place. That is the essence of MLG: fit over fidelity, motion over mandates, signal over doctrine.

## The shared pattern

Neither Amazon nor Microsoft follows the MLG model by name, but both demonstrate its core principles in action:

- **They act on signal before it becomes consensus**. Both companies have a track record of moving early – identifying shifts in market behavior or customer needs and responding before those patterns become obvious to competitors. AWS and Copilot are clear examples: built not from vision decks, but from real-time signal observed at the edge.
- **They decentralize execution to teams close to the customer**. Instead of forcing decisions through central hierarchies, they empower small, cross-functional teams to own initiatives end-to-end. Amazon's two-pizza teams and Microsoft's product-group autonomy enable faster cycles of

sensing, testing, and adapting – without waiting for top-down approval.

- **They adapt their GTM structures based on how different segments actually behave**. Rather than treating GTM as a fixed doctrine (e.g., 'we're PLG' or 'we're enterprise sales'), both companies build flexible commercial architectures that vary by audience. Microsoft's mix of self-serve, enterprise sales, and partner-led distribution across Azure and Office is a prime example of dynamic GTM in action.

- **They treat capital and resources as fluid, not fixed**. Investment follows momentum. Projects that gain traction are resourced quickly; those that stall are wound down without drama. This approach prevents long-term drift and ensures that resources stay aligned with current market opportunity – not historical assumptions.

- **Their leadership focuses not on making every decision, but on enabling reflex**. Senior leaders act as system designers, not bottlenecks. They create the conditions for rapid, local decision-making – through clear priorities, shared metrics, and a culture that rewards speed of learning over certainty of plan.

Amazon and Microsoft are not edge cases. They reveal a structural truth: transformative growth rarely survives when subordinated to the logic of the core. It needs space, it needs a mandate, and it needs protection from premature convergence. Companies that attempt to graft new models onto old hierarchies – without granting real autonomy – almost always kill the very thing they're trying to create. The future is built at the edges first. Only later does it move to the center.

## From observation to architecture

What Amazon and Microsoft demonstrate – organically, if not always intentionally – is that *responsiveness can be designed*. It's not just a leadership mindset. It's a company-wide operating system. In the pages that follow, we'll break down that system: the architecture of MLG. Not as a philosophy, not as a 'motion,' but as a set of structural capabilities that allow any company – regardless of size – to operate with the same reflexes these giants have built into their DNA.

Neither company has escaped the constraints of scale. Planning remains partially centralized. Not every investment is signal-led. Both have made costly missteps – Amazon in healthcare and retail expansion; Microsoft in mobile – when they deviated from signal or pushed unvalidated ideas. But their strongest strategic outcomes have come when they acted in alignment with MLG principles: sensing early, adapting fast, and letting execution happen close to the edge.

The rest of this chapter unpacks what the MLG framework is in detail. We'll break down the structural foundations of MLG – the core capabilities that allow any company, not just tech giants, to operate with this level of speed, precision, and fit.

## The perpetual PMF loop

Microsoft and Amazon help us understand that the defining characteristic of MLG is not market insight – it's **operating mindset**. Traditional companies may know their markets are changing. Many even collect the right signals. But few have the systems required to turn that signal into coordinated, company-wide response. They are still built to plan, not to adapt.

MLG companies operate differently. Their core motion is the *Perpetual PMF Loop*, as shown in Figure 8.

This is not a linear process, it is a metabolic rhythm, it happens continuously, at multiple levels of the organization, often in parallel. It doesn't require central approval, it requires distributed capacity.

**Sense**

Detect changes in buyer
behavior, usage patterns,
sentiment, or signal.

**Scale**

If it works, double
down. If it fails, log the
learning and kill it.

**Perpetual
product-
market-fit
(PMF) cycle**

**Interpret**

Understand what those shifts
imply for your positioning,
pricing, product, or motion.

**Test**

Run the smallest
version of the idea that
proves or disproves it.

**Adapt**

Make changes. Quickly.
Offer structure, copy, GTM
motion, pricing.

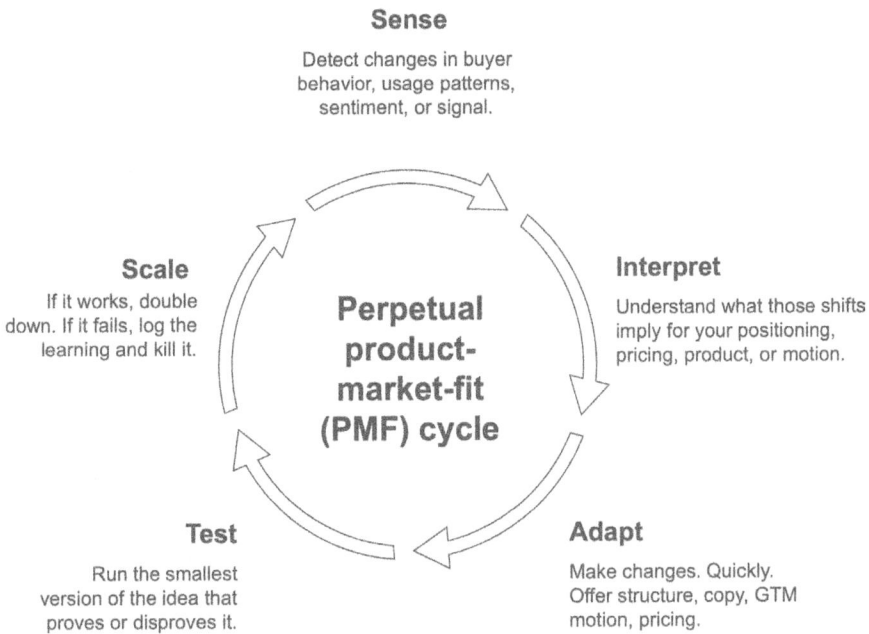

**Figure 8**  This loop is the defining model for success in the AI era, based in the recognition that PMF is a moving target, not a static location.

- **Sense**: Stay close to the market. Notice what's changing – customer behavior, competitive dynamics, friction in the funnel. Signal rarely arrives as certainty. It starts as noise. MLG organizations are built to listen.
- **Interpret**: Turn raw input into shared understanding. Patterns are surfaced, not handed down. Teams converge around what the signal might mean – not just for today's execution, but for tomorrow's fit.
- **Adapt**: Make adjustments – fast. Offers shift. Messaging sharpens. Teams reorient. The changes might be small, but the reflex is structural. The organization moves because the market moved.
- **Test**: No adaptation is assumed correct. It's tested – deliberately, visibly, and soon. Not to prove a thesis, but to learn what the market affirms. Feedback loops tighten. Waste decreases.

- **Scale**: Validated moves don't sit idle. They're codified, resourced, and extended – until they're overtaken by the next signal. Fit is not found once. It is continually re-earned.

In MLG organizations, this loop doesn't live in a strategy slide, it lives in the calendar, the systems, and the operating cadence, it is how pricing changes are proposed. How product ideas are validated. How GTM plays are refined. The loop is the heartbeat – and everything else is designed to support it.

## The five pillars of Market-Led Growth

Too many companies respond to market pressure with isolated fixes: a rebrand, a pricing tweak, a new growth team. But without systemic change, these moves are cosmetic. They don't address the root issue: a mismatch between how the company is built and how the market behaves.

MLG is a reorientation of how the business functions – organizationally, operationally, and culturally. It is what allows a company to stay in alignment with the market even as that market shifts under its feet. Over the remainder of this chapter, we'll lay out the five pillars that define this model. Each one represents a structural capability that enables speed, signal-responsiveness, and commercial adaptability. Together, they form the foundation for companies that don't just navigate change, but grow through it.

- **Shared market intelligence stack**: A system for continuously capturing, synthesizing, and distributing real signal across the organization – so that everyone operates from a common view of where the market is moving.
- **Market pods**: Small, cross-functional teams that own a defined segment or territory, with the autonomy and mandate to adjust messaging, pricing, and motion based on live conditions.
- **Adaptive GTM execution**: A flexible GTM system that evolves over time – segment by segment – through fast testing, tight feedback loops, and dynamic playbooks that reflect how buyers actually behave.

- **Leadership as velocity**: A leadership posture focused not on top-down direction, but on creating the conditions for speed: clear priorities, structural trust, and decision-making pushed to the edge.
- **Adaptive capital and resourcing**: A financial model that allocates budget, headcount, and investment dynamically – based on traction and potential, not historical plans or internal politics.

Running across all five pillars is a foundational enabler: *AI-driven execution*. When integrated effectively, AI augments every part of the system – from surfacing signal and generating insights, to accelerating adaptation and reducing the cost of execution.

## Shared market intelligence stack

### The problem: Missing signals

You cannot adapt to market shifts you haven't detected. Most companies today are structurally blind – not for lack of data, but because the intelligence they need is fragmented, delayed, or lost in translation between functions.

### The solution: A shared, real-time view of reality

Shared market intelligence corrects this. It is not a dashboard or a research function. It is a structural capability that allows the entire company – pods, leadership, and frontline teams – to operate from a shared, real-time understanding of how the market is actually changing. It turns distributed signal into coordinated action. Traditional systems collect market data to report on the past. MLG systems collect market signal to respond to the present.

### What counts as market signal

At the core of this capability is a shift in how companies define 'signal.' MLG companies don't just look at customer feedback or churn reports.

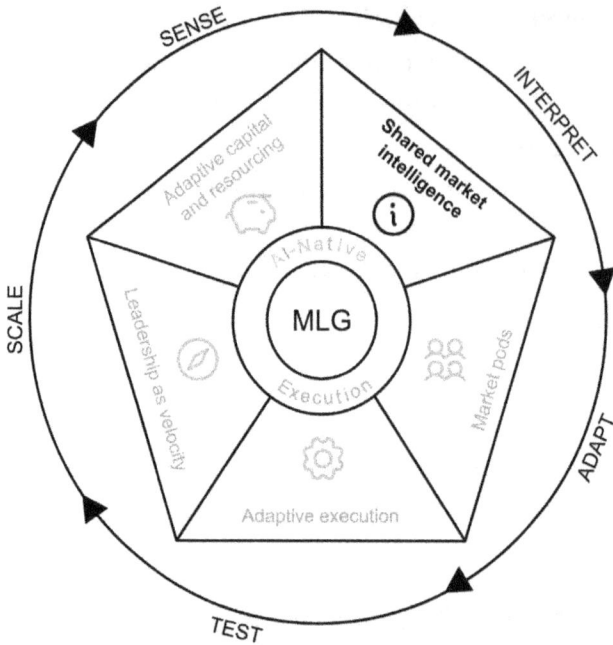

**Figure 9** It all begins with sensing what your market is thinking and demanding, and how your current product is meeting those needs and thoughts.

They pull from three overlapping signal domains – *customer, market, and behavioral* – to assemble a multidimensional picture of change. They treat customer objections, usage patterns, analyst commentary, competitor pricing changes, Reddit threads, and campaign engagement as different facets of the same thing: *live information about where product-market fit is drifting.*

No single signal in isolation is decisive. What matters is how signals combine. A single support ticket or one offhand comment in a sales call means little. But when a dip in feature usage appears alongside repeated objections from the sales teams, and a competitor quietly launches a new offer in that space, signals combine to form a single picture. Insight doesn't come from volume, it comes from triangulation.

## Weak signals matter more than you think

This is where most organizations fail. Their systems are tuned to prioritize certainty: statistically significant results, large samples, high-volume metrics. Weak signals – by definition – don't pass that test, so they get ignored. But in fast-moving markets, the first signs of change are always weak. By the time a trend becomes obvious, it's already too late to lead it.

MLG organizations are structured to act on faint signals early. They look for movement, not just magnitude. They don't confuse ambiguity with irrelevance. Their systems are calibrated to ask: What's starting to shift? Where is demand trying to move? What don't we yet fully understand, but can no longer ignore?

## The shared intelligence stack

The technical enabler of this capability is the *shared intelligence stack* – a connected system of sensing, interpretation, and distribution that functions as the nervous system of the company. It aggregates structured and unstructured data from across teams: product usage, customer relationship management (CRM) notes, call transcripts, ticket tags, community threads, and more. It surfaces patterns and anomalies, and it routes insight to the people who can act on it. It ensures that a mid-market pricing concern picked up by customer success doesn't stay buried in a ticketing system, but finds its way into the hands of the pod testing a new offer structure.

When this system is in place, the organization can move in sync. Frontline teams know what the market is doing – not just what their part of it is doing. Pods can act on signal without waiting for central blessing. Leadership doesn't have to chase down insights from ten different functions – it can see what's changing and what's being done about it, in real time. The business becomes reflexive.

## *Everyone is a sensor*

The stack is only half the story, the other half is cultural. In an MLG company, everyone is a sensor. Sales reps flag unusual objections. Customer success managers (CSMs) log recurring points of friction. Product marketers track competitor positioning shifts. Engineers read forum posts. Everyone inputs signal. Everyone accesses the output.

This is not about democratizing data for the sake of inclusion, it's about building a shared reflex. Insight doesn't flow top-down or bottom-up – it flows laterally, across the organization, at the speed required to maintain relevance. It's that reflex – not a strategy slide, not a quarterly plan – that determines whether the company can execute the perpetual PMF loop in time with the market.

## *The foundation of MLG*

Without shared market intelligence, pods are guessing, leadership is flying blind, and GTM decisions are disconnected from reality. But with it, you get the one thing traditional companies can't fake: coordinated action on emerging truth.

This is the first – and arguably the most important – pillar of MLG. Everything else depends on the organization's ability to see what's changing, understand what it means, and move before it becomes obvious.

## Decentralized market pods

### *The execution engine of MLG*

In a world of perpetual PMF, speed of decision-making is a competitive advantage. But in most companies, signals from the market flow up through layers of management. Decisions are then filtered back down to teams tasked with execution, often weeks or months later. In a static market, this process is just inefficient. In a fast-moving one, it's fatal.

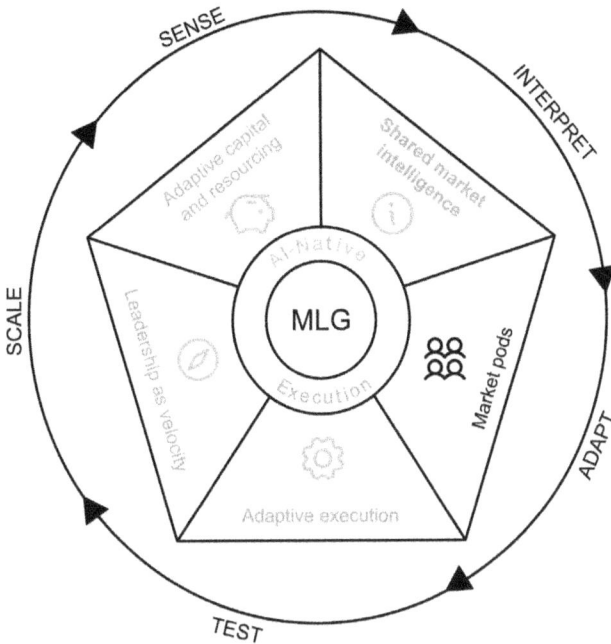

**Figure 10** MLG replaces top-down delays with decentralized market pods – so decisions happen where the insight lands.

MLG demands a different approach. The perpetual PMF loop can't function at the speed of the market if action is reserved for a central growth team or executive steering group. Execution must happen close to the signal. That's what decentralized market pods are designed to enable.

Pods are not a new flavor of cross-functional team. They are a structural shift: from linear, department-led handoffs to autonomous, segment-focused execution units that carry full accountability for adapting GTM to match changing demand. They are how the MLG system does its work.

## What a pod is (and isn't)

A pod is not a committee, it is not a tiger team, it is not a sales team with a marketer bolted on. A true market pod is a focused, cross-functional group designed around a clear scope: a specific market segment, region, vertical, or product line. Its job is not to 'run plays' assigned from the center. Its job is to generate and execute plays based on what the market is telling them this week.

Each pod includes core GTM capabilities – typically sales, marketing, product, customer success, and ops. But the defining feature isn't its composition. It's its *autonomy*. Pods don't just execute decisions – they make them. They own the Adapt → Test → Scale portion of the PMF loop for their assigned market. That might mean designing a new pricing structure, trialling a fresh messaging angle, or shifting channel mix based on behavioral signals. The critical distinction is speed: pods don't need to escalate insights to act. They have the mandate – and the tools – to adapt directly.

We'll explore the anatomy, governance, and real-world variation of pods in Chapters 5, 8, and 10. For now, what matters is understanding that this structure is not an overlay. It is the base unit of execution in an MLG organization.

## Why decision-making at the edge matters

Centralized strategy is slow. But even more important, it's imprecise. As signal travels upward, it loses fidelity. As action travels downward, it loses urgency. In most traditional organizations, by the time a signal is interpreted, debated, socialized, approved, and resourced, the opportunity that prompted it has either passed or changed shape.

Pods collapse that cycle. They remove the distance between signal and response. A pricing objection flagged in a call transcript can trigger a hypothesis, a revised proposal deck, and a test offer – launched the same week. A spike in product interest among a new buyer persona doesn't need to wait for a positioning workshop – it becomes a variant landing page and targeted outreach flow within days.

This isn't permissionless chaos, it's bounded autonomy. Leadership still defines strategy, constraints, and metrics. But within those boundaries,

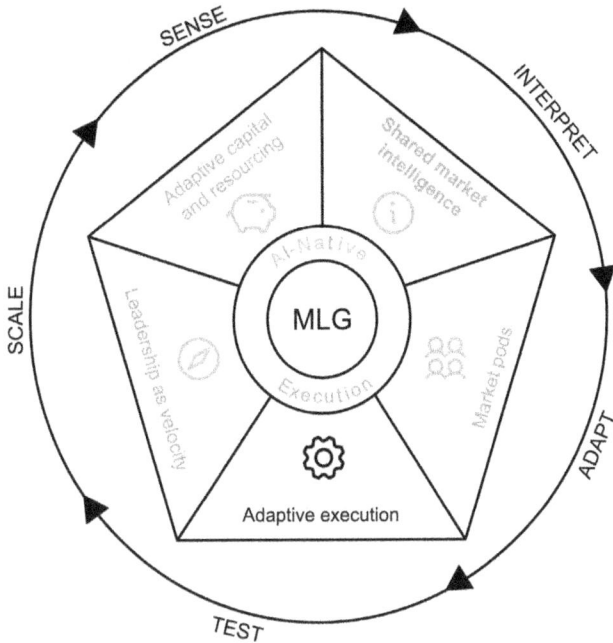

**Figure 11** MLG treats GTM as a tool, not a dogma. Each pod adapts its strategy to what the market demands – no fixed playbook, just fit.

pods operate independently. They learn faster, act faster, and iterate more effectively – not because they're smarter, but because they're closer to the truth. As we'll unpack in detail in Chapters 8 and 10, this structure also enables lateral learning. Pods don't operate in silos. They share what's working across the system – turning individual experiments into organizational intelligence.

## Adaptive GTM Execution

### *Adapting how you sell – not just what you sell*

In most companies, GTM execution hardens over time. Pricing is set annually. Messaging is standardized globally. Sales motions are templated and scaled before they're tested. Even when the product evolves, the commercial architecture around it often lags – locked in by outdated assumptions about how buyers behave.

In an MLG environment, where market fit is perpetually shifting, this kind of rigidity is a liability. A sales process that worked six months ago may now be out of step with customer expectations. A pricing model optimized for one segment may be blocking adoption in another. A self-serve funnel that once scaled efficiently may now attract the wrong profile altogether. The problem is not executional failure, it's architectural inertia.

## GTM must not become an identity

As we saw in previous chapter, clinging to GTM models as identities: 'We're sales-led,' 'We're product-led' is a mistake. These labels are treated less as design choices and more as declarations of belief. But GTM models are not belief systems. They are delivery mechanisms – tools that should be chosen, adapted, and replaced based on what the market demands.

MLG companies don't commit to a singular doctrine. They treat GTM as a dynamic system. Each pod is responsible for understanding how its market wants to buy – and adapting its commercial strategy accordingly. The question is never: 'Are we doing PLG or SLG?'. The question is always: 'What model best aligns to the current demand signal in this market, right now?'. This principle will be explored in depth in Chapters 6 and 8, where we'll look at how pods architect segment-specific GTM motions – and how leadership enables variability without losing control.

## Fit is more than product

It's not enough to have a great product. If the way you sell it is out of sync with how your market wants to buy, product-market fit will erode – regardless of feature quality or roadmap progress. Fit is a composite of product, packaging, pricing, positioning, and delivery motion, and in MLG, every one of those elements is up for revision.

Traditional organizations tend to separate monetization strategy from GTM execution. Pricing sits in finance. Packaging is managed by product marketing. Sales tactics are owned by regional leaders. The result is fragmented accountability and slow iteration. MLG collapses those functions into the market pod, and treats GTM as a dynamic system that can be tested and evolved in place.

A pod encountering hesitation on procurement calls might design a new payment model that reduces perceived risk. A sharp drop in conversion in a particular segment might prompt a shift in messaging and offer structure. None of these changes require central validation. They are local adaptations, validated through live experiments.

What matters is not consistency. What matters is fit.

## Architecture over tactics

Adaptive GTM is a structural approach to GTM execution that evolves continuously in response to market signal. It aligns how you monetize, position, and deliver your product with the current reality of customer behavior – at the pace and resolution of change.

It is built on distributed autonomy. Individual teams – whether defined by segment, geography, or product line – have the mandate and tools to adjust messaging, pricing, packaging, and motion within their domain. These adjustments are not escalations. They are the operating norm.

The system is supported by shared infrastructure: instrumentation that exposes signal, frameworks for structured testing, and mechanisms to scale validated adaptations across the organization. Change happens locally, but insight compounds globally.

Adaptive GTM is a feedback engine. Every customer interaction generates data. Every pod is accountable for turning that data into action. When the loop is healthy, fit improves, velocity increases, and execution becomes sharper over time. This is not a one-time retooling. It is an ongoing operating condition. Adaptive GTM treats responsiveness as a system capability – and builds the organizational architecture to sustain it.

## *Enabling local adaptation at scale*

None of this works without infrastructure. Adaptive GTM relies on the shared intelligence stack to surface signal, and on decentralized pods to execute tests. But it also requires leadership to create space for variance – to allow teams to run different models without seeing that as inconsistency or loss of control.

This is not a free-for-all, it's a designed system. Leadership provides strategic principles and guardrails. Pods adapt within them, signal flows upward, patterns emerge, and when a GTM variant proves successful, it scales laterally – not through top-down mandate, but through replication by informed teams.

The alternative – enforcing uniformity in the name of control – does not produce predictability, it produces brittleness. In MLG, the real work is not in choosing the right GTM model. It's in building a company that

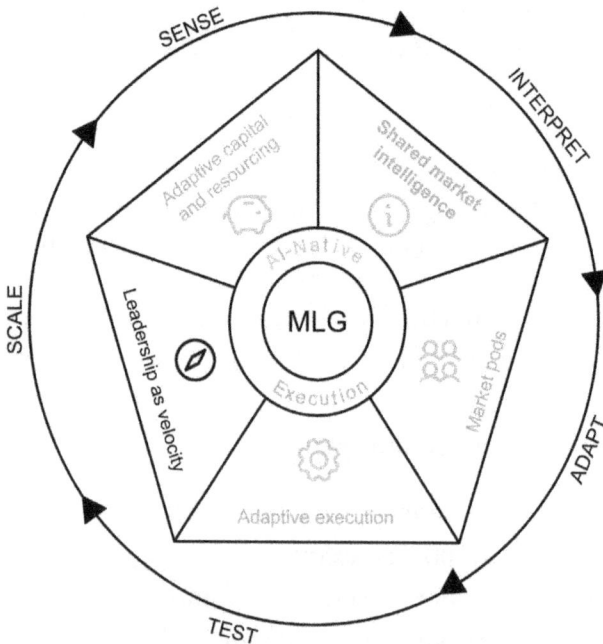

**Figure 12** MLG leaders don't make more decisions – they enable faster ones. Speed becomes structure, not slogan. Strategy stays central. Execution moves out.

can run multiple models, in parallel, and let the market decide which ones endure. We'll explore exactly how to do that in Chapter 10.

## Leadership as a velocity system

### Designing for speed, not control

In most companies, leadership is still structured around control. The assumption – implicit if not explicit – is that leaders succeed by setting strategy, approving plans, and reducing risk. But in a market that isn't going to wait for planning cycles, this model creates the very drag that holds companies back. What begins as oversight ends as unacceptable delay.

The core failure isn't tactical, it's architectural. When leaders are positioned as the final gate for decisions, they constrain adaptability to the speed of their own attention, and that speed is always slower than the market.

MLG requires a different type of leadership. One that treats speed not as a cultural value, but as a structural output. In an MLG system, leadership's primary role is not to make more decisions. It is to create the conditions in which faster, better decisions can be made by others. This is not about removing strategy from leadership. It's about relocating execution.

### Designing for systemic speed

In a high-change environment, the highest-leverage thing a leadership team can do is to build reflexes into the company. That means removing unnecessary escalation. Compressing approval cycles, reducing organizational drag. It means ensuring that a pod doesn't need to wait for a quarterly business review (QBR) to test a new pricing structure, or run a messaging variant, or shift targeting in response to new signal.

Leadership becomes a design function: not designing the playbook, but designing the system that can adapt the playbook continuously.

This shift is not theoretical, it's operational. Leaders in MLG companies take responsibility for cadence, tooling, team design, and cultural norms. They ask: How fast does signal move across the org? What gets in the way? What decisions are we still centralizing out of habit, not necessity? Where is execution slowing down – and why?

In MLG, leadership's success is measured not by how often it intervenes, but by how rarely it needs to. We'll go deeper into this shift in Chapters 5 and 6, where we'll look at the day-to-day work of building for velocity – across team structures, planning rhythms, hiring, and incentives.

## From strategy owners to system architects

This doesn't mean leaders become passive, it means they shift from being the owners of strategy execution to being the architects of strategic adaptability. They still define direction, they still set the guardrails, but they do so in a way that assumes the edge of the organization – pods, frontlines, embedded teams – will be where the majority of action happens. Their job is to ensure that those actors have the context, the trust, and the infrastructure to move without waiting for permission.

The key question is not 'How do we ensure teams don't go off course?,' it's 'How do we make it safe and expected for them to course-correct faster than we can?' This is the opposite of traditional control systems. Where traditional leadership asks, 'Is this team executing our strategy?' MLG leadership asks, 'What's changing – and is the system catching up in time?'

## The emotional work of leading fast

This shift is not just structural, it's emotional. Many leaders derive value from being the final decision-maker – the person whose sign-off confers legitimacy. Giving that up is difficult, especially when the organization has been conditioned to wait for top-down approval. But in an MLG model, those instincts slow the system down.

Leading for velocity means embracing incomplete information, distributed control, and iterative motion. It means normalizing failure – not as a sign of dysfunction, but as the price of relevance – it means being visibly willing to change your own mind in response to signal, even when it's uncomfortable.

Speed does not survive in organizations where leaders punish ambiguity, centralize power, or hide behind consensus. It survives in companies where leadership demonstrates, through action, that adaptation is not a risk. It is the job. This is *hard* – and something we'll explore more in Chapter 6.

## Culture is key

You don't get functional pods simply by drawing new org charts. The shift is cultural as much as it is structural. It requires leadership to move from control to enablement, and it requires the organization to value speed of learning more than adherence to plan.

Many companies claim to empower teams, but what they actually do is decentralize responsibility without decentralizing authority. That is not what MLG requires. A pod without the ability to execute its own ideas is not a pod – it's a dependency diagram. Making this model work takes more than reassigning headcount. It takes clear mandates, tight scopes, shared signal, and clean interfaces. It takes leaders willing to judge teams by what they learn – not just what they deliver.

Above all, it takes the humility to admit that the most accurate answers often live closer to the customer than they do to the C-suite. The result isn't chaos, it's clarity. Teams know where they're going, they know how fast they're expected to move, and they know leadership will support motion over delay. We'll unpack how to measure and manage velocity in practice – including metrics, planning tools, and review rhythms – in Chapters 6, 7, and 9.

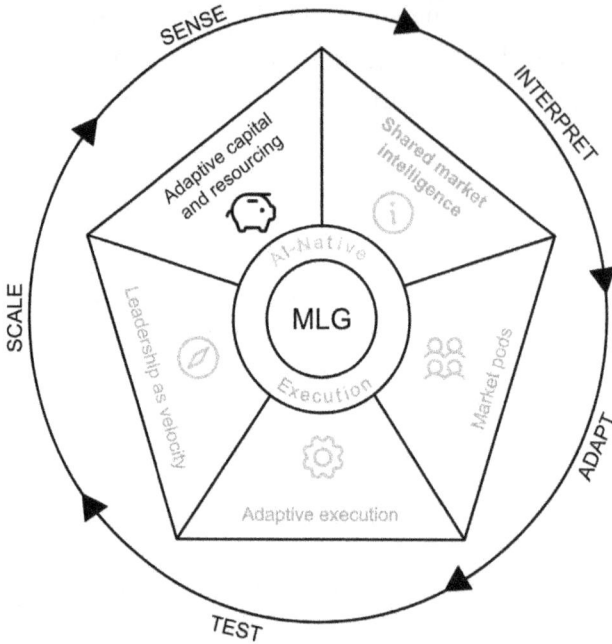

Figure 13 In MLG, budget isn't status – it's a bet. Capital flows to signal, not politics. Reallocation isn't retreat, it's how adaptive systems stay alive.

## Adaptive capital and resource allocation

### *Moving money at the speed of signal*

Most companies still allocate capital as if the market moves on a fixed schedule. Budgets are set annually. Plans are locked by quarter. Teams are funded in advance based on hypothetical performance and if they don't spend it, they lose it. The assumption is that good strategy, once approved, should be executed without deviation. Adjustments are made slowly, if at all – typically in response to failure.

The world of perpetual PMF doesn't operate on a fiscal calendar. It demands that teams adapt in real time, test hypotheses as signal emerges, and double down on traction as soon as it's validated. But most companies have no structural way to do that. Pods may identify a new opportunity, validate early pull, and still be unable to pursue it – because the budget sits elsewhere, the headcount is frozen, or the funding cycle is six months away.

The result is that resource allocation becomes linked to lagging indicators, despite being *entirely* about future performance. Teams end up over-funded to chase yesterday's strategy, and under-resourced to pursue what's working now. In effect, they're built to scale the plan, not respond to the market.

## *Money follows momentum*

In an MLG organization, capital allocation becomes reflexive. Resources flow to where signal is strongest, not where plans were previously approved. This doesn't mean chasing fads or burning through cash in the name of speed. It means structuring investment around emerging truth, not historical assumptions.

Pods that demonstrate pull – whether through demand signals, usage spikes, or early sales velocity – should be able to access incremental investment quickly. That might be budget, headcount, engineering time, or cross-functional support. Crucially, they don't need to win a political argument to get it. They need to show evidence.

Conversely, pods that are stalling don't get 'more time to prove the model.' They are wound down or re-scoped without blame. In an adaptive system, failure isn't a crisis, it's a reallocation event.

The cultural shift here is subtle but profound. Instead of treating budget as a measure of importance or status, MLG companies treat it as a bet. Like all bets, it should be adjusted in light of new information. That means leaders must reframe what it means to pull back. It's not a cut, it's movement.

We'll explore the operational details – funding models, headcount flexibility, and resourcing frameworks – in more depth in Chapters 7 and 8. We'll also touch briefly on the longer-term implications for company funding structures in Chapter 11, though the broader financial architecture of adaptive capital is beyond the scope of this book.

## Leadership as the enabler of movement

For adaptive capital to function, it needs more than intent. It needs infrastructure. Fast funding pathways. Lightweight governance. Modular headcount that can be reassigned without triggering hiring freezes or political turf wars. Shared budget pools that sit above departmental silos. Clear triggers for when and how resources move.

In traditional models, the budget process is designed to enforce discipline through constraint. In an MLG model, discipline comes from feedback loops. The system doesn't reward consistency to plan. It rewards responsiveness to reality. That means leaders must design the conditions in which resource movement is fast, safe, and normalized. Perhaps most importantly, it means resisting the instinct to protect existing spend simply because it's been committed. Sunk costs are the enemy of adaptability.

The payoff for this approach is not just faster learning or leaner spend, it's strategic clarity. Teams understand that capital is a tool for adaptation – not a reward for alignment. Execution accelerates, risk is distributed, and the organization becomes capable of scaling what works without having to first defend what doesn't.

## From fixed allocation to adaptive investment

Ultimately, adaptive capital and resource allocation is about treating money and headcount the same way MLG treats messaging, pricing, or product design: as variables to be tested, adjusted, and redeployed based on signal. Without this pillar, the rest of the system gets constrained. Pods may detect signal and propose action, leadership may want to move, but if capital can't follow fast, the reflex stalls, the moment is missed, and the opportunity goes to someone else.

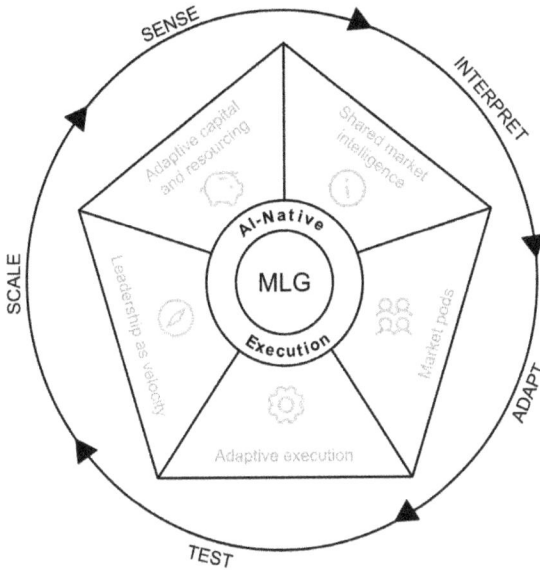

**Figure 14** In MLG, AI isn't a bolt-on – it's the engine. It makes the PMF loop faster, denser, and self-tightening. Signal becomes story. Insight becomes action.

In the chapters ahead, we'll dig deeper into how to structure for movement – without compromising accountability. But the principle stands: *you can't adapt faster than your capital moves.* MLG companies make sure it moves at the speed of signal.

## AI-native execution

### The accelerator for Market-Led Growth

Most companies today are treating AI as a tool – an assistant to help write copy faster, summarize meetings, or automate tasks in support functions. These pilots may be useful, but they miss the deeper opportunity. In an MLG system, AI is not an enhancement, it's infrastructure. It enables the system to function at the speed required by modern markets.

You can run the perpetual PMF loop without AI, but with AI, the nature of the work changes. Sensing becomes something qualitatively different. Instead of waiting for analysts to surface insights manually, AI can continuously scan usage, revenue, and engagement data to detect emerging patterns – then surface those patterns in real time, with context and narrative already attached. It doesn't just flag anomalies. It explicates their meaning.

Interpretation becomes faster and more reliable, because AI helps teams converge around hypotheses sooner – grounded in actual behavioral clusters, not gut feel or anecdote. Adaptation accelerates, because content, offers, and positioning variants can be generated and tested rapidly. Testing becomes a continuous stream, not a queue-bound project – because AI reduces the cost of iteration across design, development, and delivery.

With AI, the loop doesn't just move faster. It becomes tighter, denser, and more reflexive – embedding responsiveness not just in teams, but in the infrastructure they rely on.

### The role of AI across the loop

In a properly designed (and fully fledged) MLG system, AI supports every stage of the loop:

- **Sense**: Local (private) large language models (LLMs) continuously ingest and surface weak signals across large, noisy data sets – usage trends, sales calls, content engagement, behavioral shifts. What once took a month of analysis can be surfaced live.
- **Interpret**: It summarizes call transcripts, clusters objections, extracts themes from unstructured feedback. It flags anomalies early – before they show up in dashboards.
- **Adapt**: It enables pods to generate variant messaging, positioning angles, pricing structures, or offer formats based on the latest signal – without needing to wait for design, copywriting, or central approval.

- **Test**: It launches and monitors experiments quickly – spinning up pages, workflows, or campaigns with minimal lift. It integrates with the GTM stack to execute without a backlog.
- **Scale**: When a pattern proves successful, AI helps deploy it across other pods, segments, or channels – codifying the learning, not just sharing it.

None of this replaces the human work of framing hypotheses, applying judgment, or deciding where to focus, but it accelerates everything that surrounds that judgment. AI doesn't make strategy obsolete, it makes it operational.

## The system-level implication

Embedding AI into MLG isn't about chasing automation for its own sake. It's about lowering the cost of change. When adaptation is expensive, companies avoid it. They stick with static GTM models because retooling is slow, they delay pricing experiments because they don't have bandwidth, and they underinvest in emerging opportunities because producing the assets or workflows would take weeks.

AI-native execution removes those constraints, it makes motion cheap enough to be normal. That's what enables the perpetual PMF loop to run as a loop – not a sporadic initiative, not a quarterly reset, but a continuous operating rhythm.

We'll unpack the practical mechanics of this transformation in Chapter 9, and consider some of the second-order effects on how companies are resourced, staffed, and funded in Chapter 11. Those implications extend well beyond the remit of this book – but the directional shift is clear: *the companies that move fastest will be the ones who treat AI not as a capability, but as infrastructure.*

## Conclusion: A new operating system for a new market reality

The case for MLG is not philosophical, it is operational. The dynamics driving today's markets – faster shifts in buyer behavior, AI-accelerated competition, and tighter capital constraints – are structural. They cannot be solved with better messaging, more efficient funnels, or new org charts. They require a different kind of company.

That company is built to move. It doesn't treat PMF as a checkpoint, but as a loop. It doesn't assume that GTM is a doctrine, but a decision. It doesn't try to predict its way to relevance, it builds the reflexes to earn it in real time.

MLG is an operating system for companies trying to stay relevant in a world where the terrain shifts faster than most businesses can reorient. Its core capabilities – shared market intelligence, decentralized execution, dynamic GTM, velocity-driven leadership, adaptive capital, and AI-native infrastructure – are not theoretical ideals. They're already working, in parts and in pieces, inside the companies that continue to lead.

What's different now is that the pattern is visible, it can be named, and more importantly, it can be built – intentionally, coherently, and from first principles.

The chapters that follow will break these capabilities down. Not as abstractions, but as practical, structural changes – how you build pods, how you fund momentum, how you design leadership systems for speed. There is no universal playbook, and this is not a formula, but it is a path. You now understand the model. The rest of the book is about making it real.

# Part II

# Inside the Market-Led Growth operating system

# 4

# Shared market intelligence

## Introduction: You can't adapt to what you can't see

Most companies are not short on data, they are short on coherence. Sales hears one thing, marketing another. Product teams track feature adoption while customer success logs churn drivers. Strategy collects competitive intel, but frontline teams don't see it. Meanwhile, the CEO had a lunch with someone and now *has a hunch*. Information (of varying quality, depending on the wine at lunch) exists – but it's fragmented, delayed, and mistranslated. The result is a familiar pattern: misaligned initiatives, redundant efforts, and slow or inconsistent response to real shifts in the market.

This is not a tooling problem, it's one of structure. Most organizations were not built to detect and respond to weak signals, they are built to execute plans. When the implementation of those plans starts to generate feedback on how the market is actually moving, they lack the shared awareness – and shared mechanisms – to recalibrate fast enough.

Market-Led Growth (MLG) begins with a different assumption: the market is always moving, fit is never static, and the only way to maintain relevance is to build an organization that can detect early signs of change and respond to them coherently, across functions. That kind of responsiveness depends on a capability that most companies lack: shared market intelligence.

This is not a dashboard, it is not a research function, it is a systemic shift – from isolated insights to a common view of reality. A capability that allows pods, leaders, and teams to operate from the same live context, using the same inputs, to make faster, better-aligned decisions. In an MLG company, shared market intelligence acts as the connective tissue between signal and action. It allows distributed learning to become coordinated adaptation.

The companies that move fastest aren't the ones with the best plans. They're the ones with the clearest picture of what's changing – and the clearest mechanisms to act on that picture without waiting for executive interpretation. Shared market intelligence doesn't eliminate uncertainty. It makes the organization better at working inside it.

## From noise to signal

The shift begins with a broader definition of what counts as signal. In traditional companies, intelligence is filtered through hierarchy and reduced to reportable metrics: NPS trends, churn reports, quarterly market analyses. But these are backward-looking summaries. By the time they are compiled, contextualized, and circulated, the signal they're describing has already changed.

MLG companies treat weak signals – put together and agglomerated – as something to act on, in real time. That requires expanding the aperture – recognizing that insight lives not just in structured metrics, but in call transcripts, feature usage patterns, offhand objections, analyst notes, Reddit threads, competitor pricing pages. It lives in friction, confusion, hesitation – often faint, but directional.

Weak signals are easy to dismiss – they're anecdotal, ambiguous, and hard to quantify – but in fast-moving markets, they are the only early warning system. By the time a trend becomes obvious enough to show up in top-level KPIs, the opportunity to lead it has usually passed.

This chapter is about how MLG companies build a system to detect and respond to those weak signals. This is the first pillar of MLG because everything else depends on it. You cannot build reflexes on blind spots.

## Redefining market signal

Most companies treat 'signal' as something that arrives pre-processed: customer surveys, quarterly trend reports, dashboards of conversion metrics. But these are not signals. They are summaries – refined outputs of systems designed to report, not to enable adaptation.

In MLG, signal is treated differently – it is not a report, it is a live input – a flicker in product usage, a recurring objection in sales calls, a quiet but persistent uptick in competitor mentions. MLG companies expand the definition of signal beyond conventional boundaries – because the earliest signs of shifting fit rarely show up in polished metrics. They show up at the edge, in small patterns, buried in noise.

At the core of this shift is a recognition that market signal is multidimensional. No single input tells the full story. Insight emerges through triangulation – when multiple signals, from different sources, begin to point in the same direction. MLG companies organize market signal into three overlapping domains:

- **Customer signal**: What prospects and users say – across calls, tickets, surveys, onboarding friction, support themes, win/loss data.
- **Market signal**: What's changing in the surrounding environment – new competitors, pricing changes, analyst narratives, regulatory shifts.
- **Behavioral signal**: What users actually do – feature adoption, usage decay, funnel friction, product abandonment, usage compression across time or segments.

None of these domains alone is sufficient. A competitor's product update doesn't matter if customers don't respond to it. A sharp drop in usage may signal temporary distraction, not misalignment. But when multiple signals converge – usage declines, customers voice dissatisfaction, and a competitor launches a relevant feature – then the pattern gains weight. Insight lives in the overlap.

This approach requires a tolerance for ambiguity. Patterns don't arrive with certainty attached. But that's the point. The goal is not to reach statistical significance before acting. It's to become sensitive to the early signs of drift, and extrapolate.

MLG companies don't seek perfect clarity before they move, they seek directional confidence, and when that confidence emerges, they act – not because the data is conclusive, but because waiting for confirmation would mean arriving too late.

## Why traditional companies ignore weak signals

Weak signals are rarely ignored because they go unseen. They're ignored because the system is not built to value them. Most traditional organizations place high value on certainty. They prioritize information that is clean, quantified, and explainable – ideally with a trendline attached. Insights are expected to pass through multiple filters: standardized templates, attribution models, statistically significant samples. Anything that doesn't meet that bar is labeled anecdotal, irrelevant, or premature.

This is understandable. In stable environments, finding strong signals reduces risk. It prevents overreaction, protects resource allocation, and keeps teams aligned to long-term plans. But in fast-moving markets, this model produces the opposite effect. It slows down responsiveness, masks emerging shifts, and hardens commitment to assumptions that may no longer be valid.

Dispersion causes many signals to appear weak. Customer insights live in support tools. Sales insights are buried in customer relationship management (CRM) notes. Usage data sits with product. Competitor research lives in strategy decks. These signals don't combine – they compete. Even when teams try to share what they're seeing, they lack a common format or shared interpretive frame. A friction pattern spotted by a customer success manager (CSM) might never reach the pod building the next offer. A competitor's positioning shift might be discussed in marketing, but never make it into the sales narrative.

Most companies are trained to treat ambiguity with suspicion. If a signal isn't backed by volume, it's considered too risky to act on. If a trend can't be quantified, it's safer to defer. When a weak signal does lead to action – and that action fails – the instinct is to blame the ambiguity of the data, rather than the quality of the decision-making process.

The result is institutional deafness. Early indicators of market shift are visible, but not legible, or they're legible, but not credible, so teams wait. They wait for more data, for clearer direction, for cross-functional agreement. By the time the signal is strong enough to justify action, the cost of delay is already compounding.

MLG treats this delay as the real risk. Weak signals aren't interruptions to the strategy – they're how the market communicates its shifts. Companies that learn to detect and act on those signals early don't move recklessly. They move first.

## Signal, not noise: A triangulation example

A mid-market pod notices that win rates are falling – slowly but consistently – against a previously irrelevant competitor. At first, there's no clear explanation. But a pattern starts to emerge.

Sales begins flagging new objections: 'You're more flexible, but they're easier to buy from.' Customer success notices an uptick in pricing friction from the same segment. Product usage data shows a higher-than-usual drop-off in onboarding for accounts in that vertical. Meanwhile, a product marketer shares a post from a niche industry forum where customers are praising the competitor's new 'fast-start' offer.

Individually, none of these signals would trigger action. Taken together, they suggest the competitor has changed its packaging or procurement model – and that customers are responding. The pod repositions its entry offer, simplifies onboarding, and tests a pricing pilot. Within six weeks, conversion improves and win rates stabilize.

This is how MLG companies treat intelligence: not as isolated data points, but as early pattern recognition. The insight didn't come from one signal. It came from recognizing how several weak signals pointed to the same shift.

## The shared intelligence stack

Capturing signal is only half the challenge. The harder part is turning distributed fragments – support tickets, sales objections, product usage patterns – into something coherent. In most companies, valuable signal dies in the system. It lives in call transcripts no one reviews, in CRM notes that don't surface, in product dashboards that aren't linked to GTM decisions. Intelligence is everywhere, but insight is nowhere.

MLG organizations solve this with infrastructure. They build what we call the *shared intelligence stack* – a system of tooling, process, and norms designed to turn local observations into company-wide reflex.

This isn't a single product, it's a capability, one that sits across three layers.

## 1. Sensing

The first job of the stack is to capture signal – across functions, channels, and formats. That means pulling structured and unstructured data into one place:

- CRM notes, call transcripts, and Gong or Chorus snippets.
- Support ticket tags, product feedback, and churn reasons.
- Usage telemetry, segment-specific engagement metrics.
- Social listening, forum activity, analyst briefings, competitor web changes.

Signal collection isn't just technical, it's behavioral. Teams need to know what to log, where to log it, and why it matters. An early objection logged by a rep, a repeat complaint flagged by a CSM, a developer linking a GitHub comment to a usage drop. These are not anecdotes – they're ingredients. Everyone is a sensor, but without a system to collect their input, sensing remains balkanized.

## 2. Interpretation

Collecting signal is not enough. It must be interpreted. This is where most traditional systems stall – overwhelmed by volume or limited by manual analysis. This is where local AI becomes essential.

MLG organizations layer in lightweight, domain-specific large language models (LLMs) trained on their own internal data – transcripts, tickets, notes, telemetry – to surface patterns that no single person would catch. These LLMs can be run off an entirely local environment with tech costing US$10,000 or less, meaning each pod can run their own, where necessary – something we've detailed in Chapter 11. These models don't replace human judgment, they accelerate it. They flag anomalies, cluster themes, identify recurring language, and cross-reference behavior with feedback – giving teams a real-time, probabilistic sense of where drift is appearing.

The advantage is not automation for its own sake. It's faster pattern recognition – without requiring full certainty or consensus. When a pod sees a flagged theme emerge, they don't wait for a committee to confirm it, they act.

## 3. Routing

The final job of the shared intelligence stack is distribution – ensuring the right insight reaches the right team at the right moment. That might mean:

- Surfacing a friction pattern to a pod updating onboarding.
- Flagging a competitive move to sales enablement.
- Alerting finance and pricing teams to buyer objections in a specific region.
- Making intelligence from a high-performing pod accessible to adjacent teams considering similar moves.

Routing isn't just technical, it's organizational. The stack must know and fine-tune who gets notified, who has permission to act, and how signal is shared across pods all matter. In MLG, distribution is designed to be *lateral*. Signal doesn't just go up to leadership and wait for interpretation. It moves sideways – across the organization, with autonomy to trigger local response.

A working shared intelligence stack doesn't eliminate uncertainty. It reduces blind spots. It doesn't give you one central dashboard that answers every question. It gives you the infrastructure to ask better ones, faster, with more context. When built well, it becomes the nervous system of the company – where every part of the organization can detect change and respond in time with the whole.

## What the stack actually looks like

While every company will assemble its shared intelligence stack differently, the most effective systems are built not around specific tools, but around clearly defined layers of function.

- **Capture tools**: These include the systems where signal is generated in the course of day-to-day work – CRMs, customer support platforms, call recording tools, product analytics dashboards, internal chat logs. What matters is not just the data they store, but how easily that data can be tagged, retrieved, and integrated elsewhere.
- **Aggregation and synthesis tools**: This is the connective tissue. Tagging engines, feedback repositories, telemetry aggregators, and LLM-based assistants trained on internal data all play a role. The best systems can connect a churn comment in a support ticket to a drop in usage and a pattern of competitor mentions – without requiring three departments to build a single slide deck.
- **Routing and surfacing tools**: These determine who sees what, when. In mature stacks, signal can be automatically surfaced to pods, distributed via internal alerts or dashboards, embedded in sprint planning, or pulled into leadership reviews. These tools also allow teams to annotate and link signal to specific actions taken – closing the loop between sensing and response.
- **Knowledge capture and sharing tools**: Finally, the stack should enable shared learning. Intelligence loses value if it stays local. Some organizations build internal knowledge graphs, searchable intelligence repositories, or even simple templates for codifying and distributing signal-to-action narratives. What matters is lateral flow: making it easy for one pod's insight to become another pod's advantage.

> The point is not to install a specific tool. It's to design a system where signal flows without friction, and where patterns can emerge without requiring perfect alignment or manual intervention. This infrastructure doesn't need to be complex. It just needs to work at the speed of the market.

A shared intelligence stack is not just a technical system. It's a behavioral one. For signal to flow, people have to contribute it. That means treating every team – sales, support, marketing, product, engineering – not just as executors of strategy, but as live sensors embedded in the market.

In MLG organizations, sensing is not the job of a research team or a strategy function, it's an operational habit. Reps log the objection that feels new. CSMs flag a friction pattern they've seen three times. Product teams don't just ship features – they track usage decay and feed insight back into the shared intelligence stack to support new messaging. Engineers surface issues from forums or GitHub threads.

But the system is only as strong as the people willing to feed it, and people only feed it if they believe it leads to action. Engineers won't add what they're seeing if they think marketing doesn't care. That's why culture and tooling must reinforce each other. The organization has to reward signal detection, normalize contribution, and close the loop so contributors see what happens next. Everyone is a sensor – not because they've been told to be, but because the system makes it matter.

## Operationalizing the intelligence loop

A shared intelligence stack is only useful if it feeds execution. The point is not to 'be more informed.' The point is to act faster. That requires more than infrastructure. It requires rhythm.

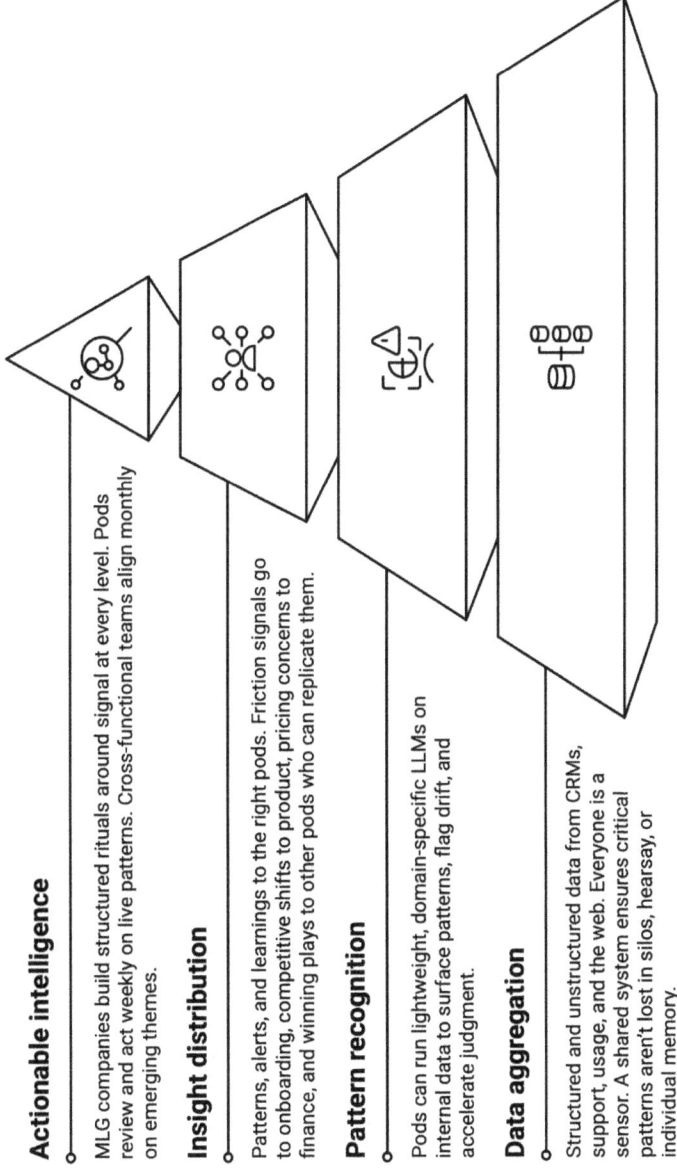

**Actionable intelligence**

MLG companies build structured rituals around signal at every level. Pods review and act weekly on live patterns. Cross-functional teams align monthly on emerging themes.

**Insight distribution**

Patterns, alerts, and learnings to the right pods. Friction signals go to onboarding, competitive shifts to product, pricing concerns to finance, and winning plays to other pods who can replicate them.

**Pattern recognition**

Pods can run lightweight, domain-specific LLMs on internal data to surface patterns, flag drift, and accelerate judgment.

**Data aggregation**

Structured and unstructured data from CRMs, support, usage, and the web. Everyone is a sensor. A shared system ensures critical patterns aren't lost in silos, hearsay, or individual memory.

**Figure 15** The shared intelligence stack turns scattered input into reflex – so local insight becomes collective advantage. Everyone is a sensor.

In MLG organizations, signal isn't handled as a special case. It's part of the operating cadence. Intelligence doesn't flow through a single quarterly deck or annual strategy offsite. It moves continuously – surfaced, reviewed, and acted on through a set of deliberate rituals that align the company around what's changing.

This loop is typically embedded at three levels.

## 1. At the pod level: Actionable signal, week by week

Market pods live and breathe the insight from the stack. Every member of the pod will be questioning it many times a day, with lightweight weekly or biweekly signal reviews. These are not research meetings, they are focused check-ins on live market patterns:

- What are we hearing, seeing, or sensing this week that's different?
- Which signals feel ambiguous but potentially important?
- What signals are we not seeing? Or is there somewhere we want more?
- What hypotheses should we test based on this?

Pods maintain a running backlog of live signals, and on this basis test ideas and offer changes. When a pattern solidifies – through triangulated feedback or behavioral confirmation – they move quickly to design a response. Pricing pilots, offer tweaks, message rewrites, or onboarding experiments are launched within the pod, without waiting for central validation.

## 2. At the cross-functional level: Shared interpretation

While pods act on localized signal, interpretation still benefits from scale. MLG firms must run monthly or quarterly cross-functional signal reviews. Again, these are not status updates. They are designed to surface broader market themes and drive convergence across pods.

In these sessions:

- Product, go to market (GTM), support, and ops teams bring their top 2–3 emerging signals.
- Discussion centers on *pattern recognition*, not resolution – what's beginning to emerge?
- Insights are catalogued centrally, then routed to relevant pods for test prioritization or offer revision.

The benefit isn't alignment for its own sake. It's avoiding duplication and enabling lateral scale – so that one pod's discovery can become another pod's advantage.

### 3.  At the leadership level: Portfolio sensing

Executives operate one level up. They use signal as a way to assess whether the product is staying aligned to the market – or beginning to drift. This means regularly reviewing not just financial outcomes, but reflex indicators: Which pods are surfacing signal and acting on it? Where is interpretation stalling? Where is signal being ignored, or overridden by legacy assumptions?

Leaders aren't expected to react to every insight. Their job is to observe the *system's responsiveness* – and step in only when reflexes degrade. When this happens, it's usually a failure of permission, clarity, or flow – not of insight.

## Conclusion: Shared signal, shared action

In an MLG system, market intelligence is not an input to strategy. It is part of the operating system. The whole goal is growth *based on what the market wants*. Market intelligence drives what pods test, what leaders review, where resources flow, and how the company adapts – not periodically, but continuously.

This kind of responsiveness doesn't require perfect clarity. It requires a different posture toward uncertainty. MLG companies don't freeze in the face of noise, they don't treat every faint signal as a directive, but they don't dismiss it either. They capture, cluster, and watch. They act when confidence becomes directional – not absolute – and they scale what works based on learning, not doctrine.

But the real power of shared intelligence is not just speed, it's coherence. When signal is visible across the organization – when the same data is interpreted, routed, and acted on laterally – adaptation can be coordinated. Pods don't duplicate work or pull in opposite directions. Product doesn't iterate while GTM repeats outdated narratives. Pricing experiments reflect real objections. Messaging shifts reflect real usage patterns. Everyone is working from the same evolving picture of what the market is doing, and what the company is doing in response.

That coherence is what separates adaptive companies from reactive ones, it's not just about seeing change. It's about turning distributed learning into unified motion. That's what the shared market intelligence stack enables. It's not a dashboard. It's not a team. It's a system – a nervous system – through which the entire company senses, responds, and evolves in rhythm with the market.

Without it, the rest of the MLG model breaks. Decentralized pods can't calibrate. GTM teams fly blind. Capital follows the wrong trends. Leadership loses the thread. But with a shared market intelligence stack, everything tightens. Reflexes align. Fit stays live. Strategy becomes what it was always meant to be: a continuous conversation with reality.

Intelligence alone doesn't create adaptability, it must be acted on. Seeing signal is one thing, responding to it – quickly, locally, and with authority – is another. That's why the next pillar of MLG is structural. It's about how companies organize to move. Because once you know what the market is telling you, the only question that matters is: Who can respond first?

In the next chapter, we'll look at the design of decentralized pods – the execution model that makes this kind of responsiveness possible at scale.

# 5

# Decentralized market pods

## Introduction: Structure eats strategy for breakfast

Most companies today understand that the market is moving faster. They know – often uncomfortably – that their organizational structure is part of the problem. Yet, when they try to respond, they reach for familiar tools: a strategy refresh, a cross-functional task force, a new analytics platform, a reorg that shifts boxes on a slide deck without changing how decisions get made. Six months later, they find themselves in the same position – moving slower than the market, wondering why nothing changed.

Here's the reality: in a world shaped by AI-accelerated innovation and continuously fragmenting demand, structure beats strategy. It doesn't matter how bold your go-to-market (GTM) plan is, or how sharp your leadership vision might be. If your organization is structurally incapable of sensing, deciding, and acting at the speed the market now demands, you are not built to survive.

Market-Led Growth (MLG) is not just a strategic philosophy. It is an operating system – a new way of building companies that treat adaptability not as an aspiration, but as a baseline requirement. It is not enough to move faster in pockets, or be more 'customer-centric' in principle. To function in an MLG model, the organization itself must be restructured for reflex. It must move from a system designed for control and predictability to one designed for continuous alignment.

This starts with decentralization. It starts by shifting sensing, decision-making, and action out of the center and into the edge of the business – into small, autonomous, cross-functional market pods that own execution for specific segments. It starts by reimagining leadership not as the approver of plans, but as the architect of conditions – creating the infrastructure, permissions, and rhythms that make fast, aligned, local response not just possible, but expected.

This chapter is about what that looks like in practice. We'll examine why traditional functional structures break down under adaptive pressure. We'll map how MLG pods work differently – not just in org charts, but in behavior. We'll also look at real-world contrasts: companies like Ford, who failed to evolve their structure in time, and companies like Bayer, who are building for adaptation from the inside out.

The future doesn't reward intention, it rewards design. Only companies built to adapt – structurally, not strategically – will be able to keep up.

## Section 1: Why traditional Org structures are built to fail in an MLG world

### The three structural failures

Three core structural problems explain why traditional organizations cannot keep up.

### 1. Centralized decision-making slows response time to a crawl

In most companies, critical decisions – pricing adjustments, GTM shifts, even basic messaging updates – must work their way up the chain for executive approval. By the time leadership reviews the data, debates the risks, and authorizes a response, the opportunity has passed. In markets moving at AI speed, centralized decision-making isn't caution. It's paralysis.

## 2.  Functional silos create internal friction that kills alignment

Sales, marketing, product, customer success – each department is optimized for its own success metrics rather than for collective adaptability. Marketing wants more leads, sales wants bigger deals, product wants roadmap stability, and customer success wants retention. No one owns the full customer experience. No one owns adaptability itself. When conditions shift, the organization doesn't move as a unit; it fights internally over who has to change first.

Sales tells marketing the leads are bad. Marketing tells sales they aren't working the leads. Product tells both that they're building based on the roadmap, not real-time feedback. Meanwhile, the competition – who aren't weighed down by these competing priorities – are executing. They're eating your lunch, and your dinner.

## 3.  Risk aversion prioritizes protecting the status quo over responding to new realities

In traditional structures, risk is a career hazard. Innovating outside your lane can be seen as reckless. Experimenting with pricing or GTM motions without full consensus is treated as a threat. The safe move – the move that gets rewarded in-house – is to keep executing the existing playbook, even as the market slowly renders it obsolete.

Clayton Christensen described this dynamic with precision in *The Innovator's Dilemma*, showing how even the most successful companies end up trapped by the very systems that once made them great. We won't try to rehash his argument here. But his fundamental insight remains critical: companies most afraid of short-term risk inevitably take the greatest long-term risk of all – irrelevance.

### Ford vs Tesla: Structure as competitive advantage

Nowhere is this failure of structure more visible than in the battle between Ford and Tesla.

Ford's mastery of mass production defined the very idea of industrial efficiency. But that same structure – one optimized to maximize throughput, minimize cost, and protect legacy processes – became a straitjacket when the market shifted toward electric vehicles (EV).

When Tesla began to gain traction with a new model for automotive innovation – vertically integrated, software-driven – a good number of people within Ford could probably see the threat clearly. But the organization *as a whole* couldn't move fast enough to respond.

- Retooling factories built for combustion engines was slow and expensive.
- Rethinking distribution models meant battling dealer networks tied up in decades of legal and financial entanglements.
- Internal champions for change were stymied by leadership structures designed to minimize disruption, not accelerate it.

Tesla operated with none of those constraints. Its structure was built for adaptability from the start. Control of design, manufacturing, software, and sales was centralized into tight loops that allowed for faster feedback and iteration. Where Ford debated five-year transition plans, Tesla launched updates over the air, changed manufacturing lines mid-cycle, and adjusted pricing dynamically based on real-time demand.

The difference wasn't vision. People at Ford saw the future. The difference was structure. Ford's organization, optimized for yesterday's world, could not execute at today's speed. Tesla's structure, designed for perpetual adaptation, could, and it did.

But structure doesn't stand still. Today, Tesla faces its own reckoning. Companies like BYD are now outpacing it in both volume and agility – building affordable EVs faster, launching new models more frequently, and mastering local supply chains in ways Tesla cannot easily match. The lesson repeats: structural advantage is temporary. If you stop evolving, someone else will build the next system that moves faster than yours.

## NVIDA vs AMD: The chip war is a structure war

We see the same structural dynamics unfolding in the AI hardware race. Nvidia has dominated the space with its H100 and GB200 chips, forming the backbone of most major AI infrastructure stacks. Its strength lies in a tightly coupled hardware-software ecosystem – vertical integration has created staggering technical performance and deep platform lock-in.

But as demand explodes, Nvidia's biggest weakness is no longer engineering – it's availability. Supply constraints are slowing deployments across hyperscalers and startups alike. Into that gap steps AMD. Their more open approach, combined with partnerships across the broader AI tooling ecosystem, allows for faster experimentation, wider distribution, and easier developer onboarding.

Meanwhile, Nvidia is adapting too. As of 2025, the company no longer builds physical prototypes for most chip iterations. Instead, it designs and tests them mostly in simulation, collapsing what was once a multi-month development cycle into a matter of weeks. The aim is clear: keep execution speed in lockstep with demand.

## Reflexes, not roadmaps

This is the hard truth: in the era of MLG, survival is not determined by who has the smartest strategy. It's determined by who has the fastest reflexes. Sensing shifts in demand, deciding how to respond, acting in the market – these must happen continuously, not sequentially. In traditional structures, each of those steps is a handoff across departments and hierarchies. In an MLG structure, they are fused into a single motion.

If you want to build a company that can survive the decade ahead, you cannot rely on structures built for a slower market. You must redesign your execution system itself.

Adaptability can't happen inside a structure built for control. It happens inside a structure built for speed.

## Section 2: The MLG solution – decentralized execution pods

### Building for decision-making at the edge

You can't simply exhort people to 'move faster' inside a system designed to slow them down. In traditional organizations, decision-making is centralized, layered, and cautious – built to protect the core, not empower the edge. In an MLG organization, by contrast, decision-making moves to the edge. It becomes the default condition, not the exception.

This isn't a cultural shift, it's a structural one. You can't empower the edge by asking nicely; you have to rebuild the organization so that sensing, deciding, and acting happen closest to the customer – without constant escalations, approvals, or handoffs.

That is the purpose of the MLG execution pod: to make decision-making at the edge not just possible, but inevitable.

### What is a Pod?

An MLG pod is a small, cross-functional, autonomous unit aligned around a specific market segment, customer type, or hypothesis. It is designed to operate as a self-contained system: sensing signals from the market, making decisions about how to respond, and executing actions – all without needing permission from centralized leadership.

Imagine a company selling a customer analytics platform. Under traditional organization, it might divide work by function – sales, marketing, product. Under MLG, it organizes around market demand and market segment instead.

- One pod focuses on mid-sized software-as-a-service (SaaS) companies looking to shift from annual contracts to flexible subscriptions.

- Another pod targets large enterprise manufacturers expanding into direct-to-consumer models.
- A third pod addresses digital media businesses pivoting toward hybrid advertising and subscription revenue.

Pods typically consist of five to ten people, blending sales, marketing, product, and customer success capabilities. Depending on the complexity of the market and customers they serve, they may also include operational or financial support. What matters is not the exact composition, but that each contains all the critical capabilities required to sense, decide, and act. Product teams stay connected through shared platforms, but market pods own how those products are adapted, sold, and supported at the edge.

Pods are not temporary project teams, they are permanent operating units, structured to own a slice of the market on an ongoing basis. Each pod is accountable for the outcomes in its domain – not for activity metrics or departmental KPIs, but for real adaptation and real results – something we'll look at more in the next chapter. In traditional structures, the GTM function is fragmented across departments. In an MLG structure, the pod becomes the atomic unit of execution.

## How decentralization drives speed without chaos

Decentralization often raises fears of chaos, inconsistency, or strategic drift, but properly structured, pods increase speed without losing alignment.

Central leadership still plays a critical role in the organization structure. Leadership sets the strategic north star: which markets matter, what boundaries pods must operate within, how success is defined. It guarantees and funds the shared infrastructure that supports all pods – data platforms, brand guidelines, financial frameworks. It acts as the systemic stabilizer, ensuring that local actions don't fragment the enterprise's broader strategic intent.

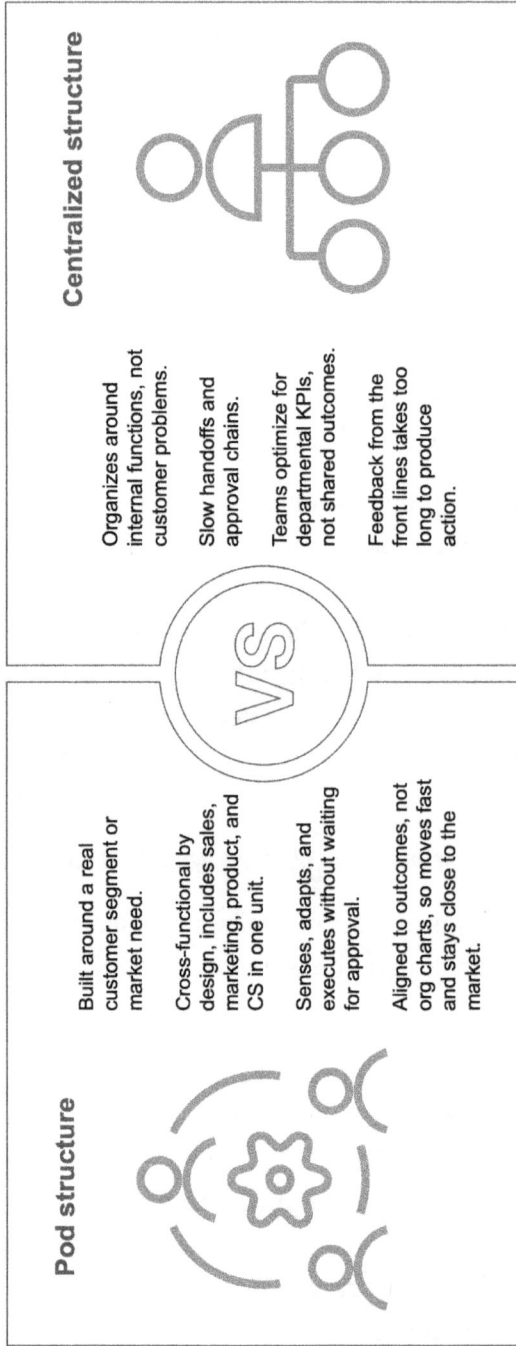

**Pod structure**

- Built around a real customer segment or market need.
- Cross-functional by design, includes sales, marketing, product, and CS in one unit.
- Senses, adapts, and executes without waiting for approval.
- Aligned to outcomes, not org charts, so moves fast and stays close to the market.

**VS**

**Centralized structure**

- Organizes around internal functions, not customer problems.
- Slow handoffs and approval chains.
- Teams optimize for departmental KPIs, not shared outcomes.
- Feedback from the front lines takes too long to produce action.

**Figure 16** Decentralized pod structure. MLG pods are autonomous, cross-functional units built around markets – not functions. They don't ask for permission, they sense, decide, and act at the edge.

What it does not do is micromanage the edge. It does not insert itself into every tactical decision. Leadership's role shifts from decision-making to velocity-enablement.

Within the strategic guardrails, pods have full autonomy to adapt their pricing, messaging, and GTM motions based on live market feedback.

- They don't have to escalate to get permission.
- They don't have to wait for cross-functional consensus.
- They do sense, decide, and act – at market speed.

This decentralized structure fuses sensing, deciding, and acting into a single, continuous motion. It transforms the organization from a chain of approvals into a network of live market engagement nodes.

## Proof in practice: Bayer and dynamic shared ownership

Bayer has always been a company of deep technical expertise, with industry-leading research and development in pharmaceuticals and agriculture. It was structured for scientific rigor and operational efficiency – but when the market shifted, that same structure became an obstacle to change.

Bayer had to rebuild its culture to enable faster, market-responsive execution. The shift wasn't just about structure – it was about rewiring the way people thought, acted, and made decisions. In mid-2024, they did just that, with what they called dynamic shared ownership (DSO).

First, Bayer empowered smaller teams closer to the coalface to make real-time decisions. Bayer dismantled its functionally siloed GTM approach and created multi-disciplinary pods focused on market segments (e.g., digital health, crop science, and pharma supply chain). Instead of waiting for corporate headquarters to approve everything, market-focused teams gained more autonomy to adjust pricing, promotions, and sales strategies on the fly.

Second, Bayer trained teams to use AI-driven fluid analysis instead of relying on static, annual strategic plans. Instead of operating on long-term forecasting models that assumed the future was predictable, teams started using real-time data to inform decision-making.

Most importantly, Bayer embraced a fail-fast mindset. In the past, failure was seen as a problem to avoid. But in an adaptive company, failure is a signal – a data point that helps the company learn and adjust faster than competitors. Teams were encouraged to test hypotheses quickly, take risks, and iterate based on results.

To reinforce this, Bayer committed to no compulsory redundancies before the end of 2026, ensuring employees felt safe taking calculated risks. Because if people believe failure will cost them their job, they will avoid taking risks altogether – and adaptability dies.

This shift didn't just change processes – it changed mindsets. People at every level of the organization started thinking in terms of speed, iteration, and market response, rather than control, precision, and risk mitigation.

At the time of writing, it's too early to see the results, but this pivot by Bayer is both radical and necessary and has shaken up how they are approaching their key markets in crop-tech.

## Section 3: The pod as the atomic unit of MLG

In an MLG organization, the pod is not a workaround, it is the design principle.

- Instead of building hierarchies optimized for control, you build networks optimized for speed.
- Instead of creating centralized expertise that filters decisions, you create local expertise that makes them.
- Instead of managing by plans, you manage by signals – and trust the pods to act.

Just as cells are the basic building blocks of living organisms, pods are the building blocks of an MLG company. Each one senses, adapts, and executes at the edge, continuously, autonomously, and in alignment with the broader strategic direction.

If you want to move at the speed of the market, you can't manage from the center. You have to *design for decision-making at the edge*, and pods are how you do it.

### Redefining the center – what moves into the pod, and what stays outside

#### *The pod is the new center of execution*

In an MLG organization, the traditional center of gravity – the corporate headquarters – no longer holds executional power. Leadership still matters, but it is no longer the default locus of action. Instead, the market pod becomes the true center of execution.

Sensing, decision-making, and acting no longer move upward through layers of management before reaching customers. They happen continuously inside the pod, at the edge of the organization, where the signals are freshest and the stakes are clearest.

The role of the corporate core shifts fundamentally. It no longer commands and controls every major decision. Instead, it builds and maintains the systems, intelligence, and strategic guardrails that allow pods to operate at speed, sustainably and in alignment with the company's overall goals. MLG is not a rejection of centralization altogether. It is a redefinition: it *centralizes platforms and principles, while decentralizing action and adaptation.*

### What moves inside the pod

In an MLG structure, the pod is no longer just a project team or a local sales unit. It is the atomic unit of business execution. Inside each pod now lives:

- **Sensing capability**: Each pod is connected directly to live customer signals – feedback, objections, opportunities, shifting behavior patterns.
- **Decision-making authority**: Pods are empowered to adjust pricing, messaging, and GTM tactics in response to what they learn, without waiting for executive approval.
- **Execution capability**: Cross-functional teams inside the pod can act on those decisions immediately – aligning sales, marketing, product feedback, and customer success actions without internal delays.
- **Responsibility for outcomes**: Pods own real commercial goals – pipeline generation, customer acquisition, expansion, and retention in their assigned market domain.
- **Continuous feedback loops**: Every market insight, success, failure, and customer signal is immediately available to both the pod and the wider organization through shared intelligence systems.

The pod is not dependent on HQ to react to the market. It is *self-contained, self-correcting,* and *directly accountable.* Execution no longer lives in functional departments scattered across the organization. It lives inside the pod.

## What stays outside the pod

Even as pods become the new centers of action, certain systems must remain outside individual pods – centralized to maintain coherence, stability, and strategic alignment.

Outside the pod remain:

- **Strategic direction**: Leadership still defines which markets the company prioritizes, what success looks like, and how resources are broadly allocated.
- **Shared intelligence stack**: AI platforms, customer data lakes, and analytics tools remain centralized, ensuring all pods operate from the same rich, real-time information base.
- **Brand guardrails**: Core brand values, messaging tone, and compliance boundaries are preserved centrally to prevent market fragmentation.
- **Corporate infrastructure**: HR systems, finance controls, legal compliance processes, and security operations remain the company's shared backbone.
- **Resource pools**: Financial capital, technology resources, and specialized expertise are pooled centrally, available for dynamic allocation across pods based on performance and need.

These centralized functions exist not to control pod activity but to *support and amplify* it. They provide the stability that allows pods to move fast without spinning out of alignment.

The distinction is simple: *Centralization strengthens what needs to be consistent. Decentralization strengthens what needs to adapt.*

## The new mental model: Pods as the core, HQ as the platform

The MLG organization flips the traditional hierarchy. The pod becomes the core unit of business activity. The corporate center becomes the platform that enables pods to operate better and faster.

The corporate core is no longer the bottleneck through which every decision must pass.

It is the platform – the infrastructure, the strategic road-mapper, the intelligence sharer. The pods are the applications – continuously evolving, interfacing directly with the environment, and delivering value at the edge.

Neither system can survive without the other, but in MLG, the center of execution is unmistakable. It's the pod, not the boardroom.

## Centralizing platforms, decentralizing action

MLG requires a company to be clear-eyed about where power must live. Platforms and principles must remain centralized to keep the company coherent and capable of scaling intelligently. Execution and adaptation must move into the pods, where they can happen at the speed and fidelity the market now demands.

Leadership's role transforms from *controlling decisions to designing and maintaining systems* that make fast, distributed decision-making possible. We'll look at that more in Chapter 6. For now, the key takeaway is that in an MLG company, execution is no longer headquartered, it is everywhere the customer is.

## Why decentralization increases speed and alignment

The assumption that centralization protects consistency has been persistent. In practice, centralized decision-making introduces delay without guaranteeing strategic coherence. Signals from the market are filtered upward through layers of management, debated by teams with internal incentives, and acted on only after opportunities have narrowed or disappeared.

MLG organizations resolve this failure not by eliminating leadership (although I'm sure we've all had that desire at some point in our lives), but by restructuring decision-making. Decentralization, properly executed through pods, simultaneously increases both speed and external alignment. Sensing, deciding, and acting become fused into a single continuous motion, tied directly to customer needs rather than internal consensus.

## Speed through structural change

Traditional organizations move slowly because their structures separate observation from decision from execution. Each requires a handoff. A signal detected by a frontline team becomes a discussion at a management level, then a strategic debate, and finally an action plan. Every transfer introduces friction.

MLG pods collapse this sequence. The same unit that senses change owns the decision and the response. The need for escalation disappears. Action is tied directly to the recognition of change, compressing cycle times dramatically. Speed in this model is not the result of exhortations to 'work harder/longer.' It is a function of removing structural drag.

## Alignment through external focus

In traditional structures, alignment is treated as an internal exercise: reconciling departmental objectives, managing cross-functional dependencies, settling conflicts between competing resource demands. As organizations grow, more energy is spent achieving internal consensus than aligning with external conditions.

In an MLG structure, alignment is external by design. Pods align themselves to customer reality because that is the reference point for their success. They are not judged by how well they align with another department's priorities but by how effectively they serve their market segment. *The market replaces the internal meeting room as the arbiter of alignment.*

The single frame of reference, kept in focus through the shared intelligence stack, allows any pod to counter leadership 'hunches' or 'ideas' with a simple question – does the data we *all* rely on, support it?

### The new role of leadership

Decentralization does not mean the absence of leadership. It is a different form of leadership: one focused on enabling, not controlling.

Leaders in an MLG organization are responsible for setting strategic direction, building and maintaining shared intelligence systems, ensuring brand coherence, and providing the infrastructure that allows pods to operate independently. Their effectiveness is measured not by the volume of their decisions but by the speed, coherence, and effectiveness of pod-level execution.

Leadership becomes an exercise in system design rather than tactical approval. It requires clarity, discipline, and a willingness to cede tactical control in exchange for greater systemic velocity. We'll talk more about that in Chapter 7.

## Conclusion: Build reflexes or be left behind

Speed and alignment are not opposing forces. In an MLG organization, they are the result of the same structural shift: moving decision-making to the edge and tethering it directly to the market. Organizations that cling to centralized models in the name of consistency will achieve neither speed nor coherence. Those that decentralize intelligently will move faster, learn faster, and align themselves more tightly to the evolving realities of their customers.

Companies rarely fail because they misunderstand market shifts. They fail because their structures prevent them from responding in time. Recognition is not enough. In a world moving at AI speed, survival depends not on strategic awareness but on structural reflexes – the ability to sense, decide, and act before opportunity windows close.

Organizations that preserve centralized control will experience a consistent pattern of decline. Signals will be lost or slowly climb the hierarchy. Decisions will lag, bogged down by internal negotiations. Strategic plans will drift away from reality as customer needs shift faster than leadership can respond. Internal politics will replace external focus. High-agency employees will leave first, accelerating organizational decay. Competitors with faster reflexes will capture demand before slower companies can react.

Ford recognized the importance of electric vehicles early. It had the resources and the brand strength to compete. However, its structure – optimized for mass production and centralized decision-making – slowed its response. Tesla moved faster, iterated faster, and defined the EV category before Ford could adapt. The gap was not strategy, it was reflex.

MLG demands structural adaptability, not just strategic awareness. Organizations that delay decentralization in the hope of preserving traditional control will not buy time, they will lose relevance. In MLG, survival is not about waiting for clarity. It is about building systems that react to high uncertainty as fast as possible. The choice is not between control and chaos. It is between building reflexes that help you navigate what *looks* like chaos – or being left behind.

# 6

# Adaptive go-to-market execution

## The GTM success paradox

Today, when something starts to work in one part of the business – a new pricing model, a sharper message, a restructured offer – the instinct is often to scale it, quickly. Central teams take the success, package it into a playbook, and issue a directive: 'This is the new standard.' Rollout begins. Enablement sessions are booked and templates are pushed to the field.

But something strange happens. The same model that worked so well in one team or market underperforms elsewhere. Conversion doesn't improve. Sales velocity stays flat. Teams execute the playbook, but the results don't follow. What felt like a breakthrough fades into background noise. People revert to type – while grumbling about 'corporate' getting in the way. This isn't because the insight was wrong, it's because scaling stripped away the conditions that made it work.

The paradox is this: the more aggressively you try to scale success, the more likely you are to kill it. In Market-Led Growth (MLG), scale isn't about rollout, it's about recognition. What works is allowed to echo – across segments, across pods, across time – because it remains alive to its context. Scale will come organically and sustainably, as you let this play out. Pods themselves scale (and collapse) this way too – but that's a whole other chapter (Chapter 12, for those who want to skip ahead).

But the truth is that most go-to-market (GTM) innovations are context-sensitive. A new message lands because it responds to a specific buyer hesitation. A pricing model gains traction because it aligns with a certain procurement dynamic. An onboarding variant succeeds because of the timing, tone, or segment. When these innovations are extracted from that context and turned into generalized best practices, they lose fidelity – and with it, impact.

MLG takes a different approach. In MLG, scaling happens laterally, not hierarchically. When a pod discovers something that works, it doesn't trigger a corporate rollout, it creates a signal.

That signal is shared – through internal communities, intelligence systems, or informal storytelling. Other pods can pick it up, assess its relevance, and adapt it to their own conditions. Adoption is not mandated, it's earned. Patterns emerge across pods – not because they were enforced, but because they proved useful in practice. Success spreads the way it spreads in a functioning market: by delivering value, not by being declared universal by a central core.

The role of leadership here is subtle but critical. Not to codify prematurely, but to amplify promising patterns. To ensure the signal travels without flattening it into policy too soon. Standardization has a place – but it comes after repeated replication, not before.

## GTM is not an identity

This is a foundational shift, because most companies don't just choose a GTM model, they adopt one as a kind of identity. 'We're product-led,' 'We're enterprise sales-led,' 'We win with partner co-sell.' These aren't treated as temporary configurations. They become belief systems – reinforced in culture decks, hiring profiles, and internal shorthand. Over time, they shape how strategy gets made, which voices carry weight, and what types of execution are considered legitimate.

This identity-driven approach is understandable, it creates clarity, it signals intent to investors and employees, it gives focus to execution, but it also creates rigidity. When market dynamics shift, these GTM identities can become liabilities. Teams cling to familiar motions even when they stop working. Product teams keep optimizing the self-serve flow while customer acquisition stalls. Sales leaders double down on outbound even as buyer responsiveness declines. The organization doesn't stop executing – it just keeps executing the wrong model.

MLG treats GTM not as an ideology, but as a delivery system. A means of getting value to the customer in a way that aligns with how they actually want to buy. The role of the company is not to commit to a single doctrine. It's to continuously ask: What model best fits the current buyer, in this market, right now?

This reframing unlocks a different kind of adaptability. One pod might discover that layering outbound sales on top of a product-led motion accelerates enterprise adoption. Another might pivot from usage-based pricing to simple tiers after seeing confusion in procurement. A third might find that bundling features for a newly emerging persona unlocks a stalled segment. None of these require a wholesale change in strategy. They're local adaptations – responses to local signal.

In a traditional GTM model, this kind of variation is often treated as inconsistency. In MLG, it's expected. The goal isn't to pick the right doctrine and enforce it. The goal is to run multiple models in parallel, with enough strategic coherence to enable pattern recognition – but enough local autonomy to allow for fit. Because what wins in one segment or geography may not work in another, and what worked last quarter may not work tomorrow.

## Execution falls behind the market

In most organizations, GTM systems are designed to execute – not to adapt. Pricing is set annually, if not less often. Messaging is updated on a quarterly cadence. Sales motions, once operationalized, become embedded as training programs and customer relationship management (CRM) workflows. What begins as a sensible effort to bring consistency to execution eventually calcifies into rigidity. As the product evolves, as the customer changes, as the market shifts, the commercial architecture wrapped around the product remains stuck in past assumptions.

This decoupling of product from delivery system is dangerous because execution lags silently. It often takes months of declining conversion, shrinking sales velocity, or customer churn before the problem becomes visible, and even when the issue is spotted, the mechanics of change are slow: new collateral must be built, sales must be retrained, pricing must be modeled, approved, rolled out. By the time GTM adjustments are live, the market may already have moved again.

Companies rarely treat this as a systemic issue. The default assumption is human failure: poor sales execution, bad messaging, underperforming segments. But in reality, teams are often executing precisely what they were asked to – just on an outdated blueprint. The problem isn't tactical underperformance, it's architectural inertia.

MLG treats this differently. It starts from the premise that GTM 'fit' is never fixed. That the way customers want to buy changes more quickly than most companies can react. That execution systems must be built to adapt continuously – not just through annual planning or post-mortems. In MLG, GTM is not a machine that runs – it's a system that evolves – because (once more for those at the back) product-market fit (PMF) is not an achievement, it's a moving target.

## Fit is more than product

In most organizations, PMF is treated as the ultimate benchmark. If the product is good enough – if it solves a real problem, delivers measurable value, and scales technically – then revenue should follow. However, in practice, many companies with strong products struggle to grow, deals stall, activation lags, churn creeps upward, the instinct is to look back at the product. However, the problem often lies elsewhere: not in what's being built, but in how it's being brought to market.

What matters is not just product-market fit – it's *model-market fit*. A great product packaged and delivered in the wrong way will underperform. A merely adequate product, when framed and priced correctly, can thrive. Fit, in this broader sense, is a composite:

- **Product** – what you build.
- **Positioning** – how it's framed to buyers.
- **Pricing** – how value is exchanged.
- **Packaging** – how the offer is structured.
- **Delivery motion** – how it's sold and supported.

Each of these elements must align with how the customer actually wants to buy. If the pricing model introduces risk or friction, adoption will stall. If positioning doesn't resonate with the buyer's mental model, urgency evaporates. If the sales motion feels misaligned – too heavy-touch for self-serve buyers, too light-touch for complex deals – credibility suffers. Misalignment in any of these areas weakens fit, even if the product itself is sound.

Traditional GTM structures are poorly equipped to address this. Pricing lives with finance. Packaging is owned by product marketing. Sales process is set by regional leadership. Positioning is crafted at the brand level. The result is fragmentation: a GTM wrapper stitched together from disconnected assumptions, built by teams who often operate in parallel rather than in sync.

MLG collapses these decisions into the pod. Instead of waiting for central functions to iterate through quarterly planning cycles, pods evolve their own model-market fit in real time. They test different framings, explore alternative price points, and adapt delivery motions based on direct feedback and observed behavior. When something doesn't land, they don't escalate – they experiment – and when something starts to work, it becomes the basis for further refinement.

In MLG, model-market fit is not a static achievement, it is a dynamic system state – something you are always tuning, always testing, always evolving. It's also something you have multiple variations of *inside the company itself*. You don't have *just one*.

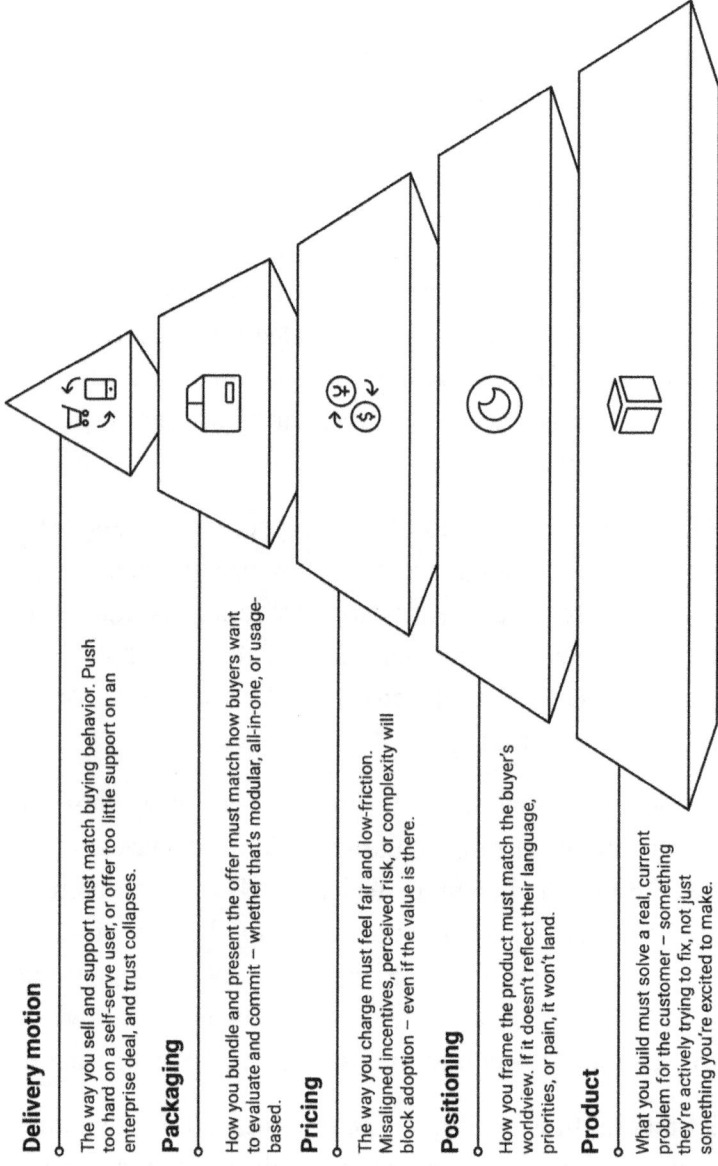

**Delivery motion**

The way you sell and support must match buying behavior. Push too hard on a self-serve user, or offer too little support on an enterprise deal, and trust collapses.

**Packaging**

How you bundle and present the offer must match how buyers want to evaluate and commit – whether that's modular, all-in-one, or usage-based.

**Pricing**

The way you charge must feel fair and low-friction. Misaligned incentives, perceived risk, or complexity will block adoption – even if the value is there.

**Positioning**

How you frame the product must match the buyer's worldview. If it doesn't reflect their language, priorities, or pain, it won't land.

**Product**

What you build must solve a real, current problem for the customer – something they're actively trying to fix, not just something you're excited to make.

**Figure 17** Model-market fit pyramid. PMF isn't enough. MLG optimizes for model-market fit – aligning product, pricing, packaging, and motion to how customers actually want to buy.

## Adaptive GTM is a system, not a tactic

And that is *really important*. It's a *system*, not something you do once, or every now and then. This is a bigger shift than you might think. When companies talk about improving GTM, they often default to tactics: a sharper pitch deck, a refreshed website, a new outbound cadence.

Adaptive GTM begins from a different premise. It treats GTM not as a fixed machine to be optimized, but as a living system to be evolved. That means positioning, pricing, packaging, and delivery aren't one-time decisions. They are components of a system designed for revision. The point isn't to find the perfect model and roll it out universally. The point is to build a system that can tune itself – locally, continuously, and based on real buyer signal.

In practice, that system lives in the market pod. Each pod owns not just execution, but commercial design. That includes how the product is positioned, what the offer includes, how it's priced (both the cost itself, and the model – transaction, subscription, usage, dynamic), and which channels or motions are used to deliver it. This autonomy is not about decentralization for its own sake. It's that the best way to discover what works in a given segment is to allow the team closest to the customer to test and evolve the model in place.

The system is designed to enable local variation within global guardrails. While leadership ensures coherence across the company, the pods control the fine-tuning. They're not waiting for new marching orders. They're adjusting the system as they go.

That's the critical shift for teams: from executing a plan to evolving a system. From optimization to adaptation. In MLG, GTM isn't a campaign or a program and is definitely not gospel. It's a dynamic interface with the market – one that can change week to week, pod to pod, based on what the customer is actually telling you.

## Learning is the execution loop

In most companies, learning is something that happens after the fact. A quarterly business review (QBR) highlights a drop in conversion. A win-loss analysis flags issues with positioning. A strategy offsite resets direction. These are all lagging rituals – well-meaning but structurally late. The damage has already been done, and recovery depends on slow cycles of diagnosis, alignment, and rollout.

MLG flips this logic. In MLG, learning isn't retrospective, it's operational. The execution loop *is* the learning loop.

That means learning is not just something you do – it's the way you work. Pods observe signal, design a response, test it live, and course-correct fast. The system doesn't need to pause to reflect. It reflects *in motion*. This kind of real-time reflexiveness depends on three principles.

### 1. *Speed over certainty*

Most organizations are wired to seek confidence before acting. The result is delay. By the time a change has been researched, validated, socialized, and approved, the opportunity has often shifted – or disappeared.

MLG pods bias toward action. They operate under the assumption that fast, imperfect action is better than slow consensus. They don't wait for 95% confidence. They move, design lightweight tests, and learn through doing.

- A pod sees procurement and then spins up a limited-scope pricing variant the same week.
- A new segment shows interest and then launches a tailored landing page before committing full support.

This isn't recklessness, it's tempo. In adaptive GTM, speed reveals strategy.

## 2. Learning velocity

What separates high-performing pods isn't how much they know. It's how quickly they learn. The faster a team can generate, test, and internalize new hypotheses about its market, the better it adapts over time.

Gains compound, a pod that runs three pricing experiments in a quarter learns more – *and faster* – than a pod that runs one well-researched initiative a year. Insights from one experiment spark ideas for the next, and when signal is shared laterally across pods, the whole system accelerates.

## 3. Immediate action

Insight without action is waste. The longer the gap between learning and doing, the less value that insight holds. MLG pods are structured to act on signal immediately.

This is where traditional teams struggle. Even when insight is generated – through customer feedback, telemetry, or sales data – it often gets lost in backlog prioritization or cross-functional dependency. By the time action is taken, the moment has passed.

Adaptive GTM collapses that delay. A pod that sees churn spike can redesign the onboarding journey this week. A pod that senses messaging fatigue can rewrite the email sequence today. Learning without action is theater. Learning *with* action is leverage.

These principles – speed, learning velocity, and immediacy – aren't just ideal aptitudes. They're design criteria. Pods must be structured to move quickly, test fluidly, and execute without waiting for central approval. Without this foundation, GTM becomes an implementation engine. With it, it becomes a live interface with the market.

## Breakout: Metrics deserve their own space

The ability to learn, test, and adapt in motion depends on one thing above all: measurement. Without clear, contextual, and actionable metrics, teams can't see what's working, where they're drifting, or how to improve. But metrics are not a footnote to adaptive execution – they are a key part of MLG. Getting them right means moving beyond vanity KPIs or lagging performance dashboards. It requires designing metrics that surface signal, enable reflexes, and fuel shared learning across pods. That's a bigger subject than we can do justice to here – and one detailed in Chapter 8.

## Conclusion: Aim for continuous commercial realignment

Most companies treat GTM as a structural decision. Once made, it sets the frame: how sales operates, how pricing is set, how marketing aligns. Over time, execution becomes implementation. GTM is no longer something the company adapts – it's something it obeys.

MLG replaces this with a different posture. GTM is not a fixed model to be rolled out. It's a living system to be tuned – continuously, locally, and in response to real signal. The work is not to perfect the architecture and enforce it at scale. The work is to build a company that can evolve its architecture as the market shifts to maintain focus and alignment with PMF and model-market fit.

This means trading rigidity for responsiveness. It means replacing static identity ('we're product-led') with situational design ('this segment responds to this motion right now'). It means trusting the teams closest to the market to make decisions – not just execute instructions. Big decisions like how to charge, what to charge, and even who to sell to, and it means building the infrastructure, culture, and leadership patterns that make adaptation possible without losing coherence.

Adaptation isn't an exception, it's the *point* of the operating system. The companies that thrive in a fast-moving market aren't the ones that execute perfectly against last year's plan. They're the ones that see what's changing, test quickly, and shift course in time. This is the core of adaptive GTM execution. Fit is always in flux. The goal isn't to chase it – it's to build a system that stays close enough to the market to move with it.

But if that's true (and let's assume it is, in this book) – then building, growing, and maintaining that system is the most important job in the business – and that's discussed in the next chapter.

# 7

# Leadership as velocity

## Leadership must change at the core

Traditional leadership models were built for a different market reality. They were optimized for stability, predictability, and control – qualities that allowed companies to operate efficiently when markets evolved slowly and competition moved on similar timescales. Leadership was about directing resources, approving plans, and minimizing risk. In a Market-Led Growth (MLG) environment, that model fails.

In MLG companies, leadership is not defined by the volume of decisions made at the top. It is defined by the ability to build systems – structural and cultural – that enable the organization to sense, decide, and act at market speed. Leadership is not about commanding individual moves. It is about engineering continuous organizational reflexes.

This requires a complete shift in mindset. Leaders are no longer responsible for knowing the right answer before the market moves. They are responsible for building organizations that can find the right answer faster than competitors once the market shifts. Control is no longer the primary asset, adaptability is.

This applies as much to financial decisions as it does to operational ones. In adaptive systems, capital cannot remain fixed. Budgeting is no longer a one-time act of judgment – it is a continuous process of alignment. Leaders must stop treating resourcing as a static plan to enforce and instead become stewards of capital flow, designing systems that allow investment to follow the signal. That shift – from episodic allocation to continuous stewardship – is one of the hardest mindset changes MLG requires. We'll return to it in depth in Chapter 9.

But in this chapter, we will define what leadership must become in an MLG company: the architect of structure and culture; the enabler of speed and alignment; the designer of reflex systems rather than the commander of plans. We will examine how structure without culture fails, how real-world companies have succeeded or faltered based on leadership reflexes, what new metrics define leadership effectiveness, and why talent strategy must shift to support adaptability as a core competence.

In MLG, leadership is not measured by the decisions leaders make, it is measured by the reflexes they build.

## Section 1: The two jobs of leadership

Leadership in an MLG company has two essential, non-transferable responsibilities: designing and maintaining the *structure* and the *culture*. Both are mandatory. Success in one without the other leads to stasis or chaos, but not adaptability.

### Structural design

The first job is structural design. Leaders must build and maintain the frameworks that allow pods to operate autonomously while remaining strategically aligned. This means setting clear market priorities, defining success through strategic guardrails, and ensuring that every pod has access to shared intelligence – data, AI-driven insights, customer signals – that inform real-time decision-making. It also means managing capital dynamically, allowing investment to flow toward pods showing real traction without waiting for annual budget cycles.

Structure, in this context, is not an org chart. It is the execution system of the company. It determines whether information flows fast enough, whether decisions are made close enough to the customer, and whether adaptation happens before market windows close. Designing structure in an MLG company demands clarity on fundamental operational questions:

- At what level do I define a market pod? Is it organized by industry vertical, customer segment, or geography?
- Should enterprise and mid-market customers be served by the same pod, or are they different enough to need two?
- Do verticals like Media and software-as-a-service (SaaS) demand separate pods due to fundamentally different buying patterns?
- What functional capabilities must live inside the pod? Do sales, marketing, product feedback, operations, and finance sit locally, or does the central platform support some functions?
- How many pods can I support with the resources I have today – and how will I know when to add or consolidate pods?
- How will I ensure access to shared intelligence, maintain brand guardrails, and allocate resource pools so that pods operate autonomously but stay aligned?

These are not questions that can be answered once during a reorganization and then forgotten. In an MLG company, structure is a living system, continuously refined as the market evolves. Leaders who treat structural design as a static exercise will find themselves running a company optimized for yesterday's demand, not today's.

## Cultural design

The second job is cultural design. Leaders must create and protect a cultural operating system where speed, adaptability, and learning are normalized. Cultural design in an MLG company is not about slogans or value statements. It is the deliberate construction of norms, incentives, and visible leadership behaviors that determine how people act under uncertain and evolving conditions. Designing culture requires leadership to confront fundamental questions:

- What behaviors do we reward explicitly? Fast iteration? Raising bad news early? Acting on imperfect information? (Answer… you should reward all of those.)
- What behaviors do we penalize? Defensive consensus-building? Risk avoidance? Political maneuvering? What does being penalized look like?
- How do we model curiosity, speed, and adaptability at the leadership level, so that they are reinforced throughout the organization? How do *you* adapt weekly?
- How do we ensure that pods operate with customer signals as the primary arbiter of action, rather than internal politics?
- Are our incentive structures tied to speed of execution, learning velocity, and market responsiveness – or still tied to static, historical KPIs?

Culture, like structure, cannot be designed once and left alone. It must be actively maintained, reinforced through incentives, examples and behaviors, and continuously recalibrated as the company scales. Leaders who treat culture as a communications exercise rather than a design challenge will find themselves leading organizations optimized around perverse incentives.

Leadership must model the behavior it wants repeated. Curiosity over certainty. Execution over debate. Learning from failure over punishing imperfection. Incentive systems must promote these values or they will collapse under operational pressure.

*When leadership neglects structural design, the company fragments. When leadership neglects cultural design, the company ossifies.* Either failure leads to the same outcome: an organization too slow to adapt to the realities of the market.

In MLG, leadership is the architect of the execution system and the steward of the behavioral system. Without both systems working in concert, adaptability decays into slogans and speed decays into chaos. Velocity requires structure. Sustainability requires culture. MLG Leadership must deliver both, or deliver neither. That is their only job.

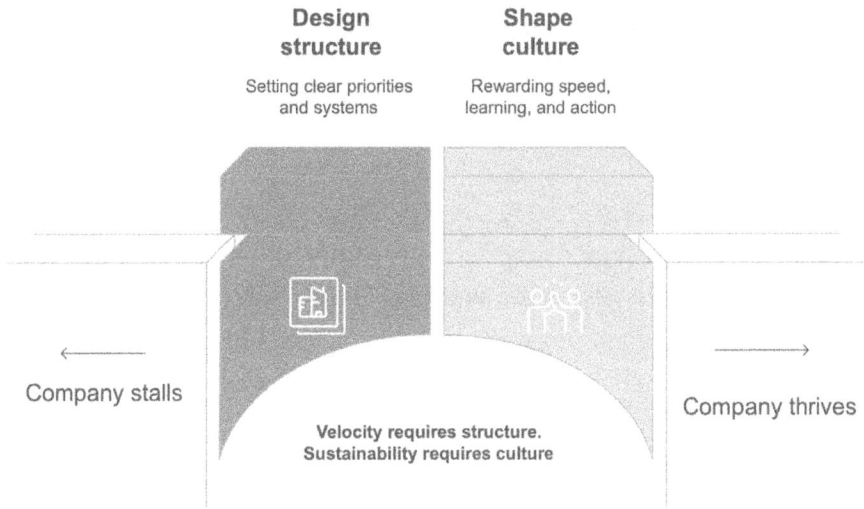

Figure 18 The new role of leadership. MLG leaders don't just set direction – they design systems. Structure enables speed, culture sustains it. Without both, adaptability dies.

## Section 2: Structure without culture fails

Structure enables action. Culture governs how people behave inside that structure. Without the right culture, even the most carefully designed systems decay into inertia, hesitation, and internal politics. Execution slows not because the framework is wrong, but because the behavioral defaults inside the framework still point toward risk aversion, protectionism, and internal negotiation.

Imagine a company that has a clear shift happening in its market. Competitors are moving faster, customers are demanding something new, and the data is unmistakable. But inside the company, the conversation is different.

One key executive refuses to budge, defending the current model they helped build – because admitting the need for change would mean admitting that their past strategy is no longer working. Another team filters and reshapes incoming data to protect their existing roadmap.

Instead of iterating, the company debates. Instead of executing, it waits for more data. Instead of adapting, it sticks to the existing plan, hoping that it will be enough. By the time the consensus shifts, the opportunity has passed.

This is not a failure of strategy, it is a failure of culture. Adaptability does not simply mean moving fast when ordered. It means building an organization where people are willing – without prompting – to shift their thinking, let go of prior assumptions, and act on new signals. The moment even a small part of the organization becomes rigid, defensive, or politically self-protective, adaptability dies.

You cannot have an adaptable organization if your culture protects egos, rewards certainty over curiosity, or allows intransigence to slow down execution. No amount of structural design can override a culture that values the wrong behaviors. Without active cultural design, structural decentralization becomes theoretical. Execution at market speed requires not just permission to act, but an expectation that action happens fast, while learning and adaptation are continuous.

Leadership's responsibility is not simply to create structural possibility. It is to continuously design, protect, and reinforce the cultural reflexes that determine how the structure operates under pressure.

The symptoms of structural failure driven by weak culture are easy to spot. Escalations remain the default mode of decision-making. Customer feedback is collected but not acted upon without executive validation. Pods execute motion without adaptation, treating autonomy as permission to replicate the plan rather than respond to the market. High-signal employees leave, frustrated by organizational inertia, while political actors thrive by managing perceptions internally rather than delivering outcomes externally.

This is the critical point: MLG is not achieved by building decentralized systems alone. It is achieved by ensuring that the people operating those systems behave in ways that maximize sensing, deciding, and acting at speed. Without cultural reinforcement, structural decentralization is a theoretical exercise – easy to map, difficult to live.

# Section 3: SAP vs Shopify – a study in leadership reflex

Structural design enables speed. But leadership reflex – the speed and courage with which leaders act on market signals – determines whether that structural potential is ever realized. Companies that recognize shifts but delay adaptation are no better positioned than companies that never saw the change coming. Recognition is not the differentiator, action is. Two real-world examples illustrate the point: SAP, where leadership hesitation paralyzed structural adaptation, and Shopify, where leadership explicitly designed the company to strengthen under market volatility.

## SAP: Protecting the past instead of building reflexes

In the 2010s, SAP sat at the pinnacle of enterprise software. Its high-margin, on-premise solutions dominated corporate IT. When the shift toward cloud computing began to accelerate – led by Salesforce, Amazon, and Microsoft – SAP recognized the trend intellectually. It launched cloud initiatives, announced product adaptations, and made acquisitions intended to accelerate the transition.

But at the leadership level, the reflexes of the organization were aligned not with adaptation but with preservation. SAP's executives, many of whom had built their careers on the success of the on-premise model, resisted any change that might disrupt near-term revenue. Strategic documents balanced cloud and on-premise priorities delicately, avoiding the hard choices required to reallocate resources, retrain sales forces, and redesign product roadmaps around SaaS realities.

The result was a series of half-measures. Cloud products existed, but were inconsistently prioritized. Migration paths for existing customers were slow and complex. New sales incentives often still favored legacy solutions. Internally, cultural inertia protected the old model. Leaders debated whether to accelerate the shift; few acted decisively.

By the time SAP fully committed to the cloud transition, the competitive landscape had changed. Salesforce dominated SaaS customer relationship management (CRM). AWS and Azure had redefined infrastructure expectations. Customers had recalibrated their buying assumptions around real-time scalability and subscription-based economics. SAP's belated shift could not close the gap.

SAP did not fail because it lacked awareness. It failed because leadership prioritized protecting the past over building and shifting with the new. In an MLG environment, structural redesign without leadership reflex is functionally irrelevant. The company still moves at the pace of its leadership's willingness to let go of the past.

### Shopify: Designing for antifragility

Shopify represents the opposite case. From its earliest years, Shopify's leadership understood that stability was not the natural state of digital markets. Rather than building a company that could withstand volatility, they set out to build a company that would strengthen under volatility. They borrowed the concept of 'antifragility' from Nassim Taleb – not resilience, not robustness, but systems that gain from disorder – and embedded it into their leadership philosophy.

This commitment to antifragility was not rhetorical, it was operationalized in real leadership behavior. When the pandemic disrupted global commerce in 2020, many companies froze, waiting for clarity. Shopify moved immediately. Leadership pushed decision-making to the edge: frontline teams extended free trials to traditional retailers going online for the first time, launched AI-powered onboarding tools within days, and deployed automated merchant support systems without waiting for formal budget cycles. Action was prioritized over perfection. Market signals dictated execution, not headquarters debates.

The same leadership reflex was visible in strategic decisions. For years, Shopify had invested heavily in building its own fulfillment network, seeking to compete with Amazon on logistics. Yet in 2023, despite significant sunk cost and revenue implications, Shopify leadership chose to offload the fulfillment business to Flexport. They recognized that operating a logistics network would reduce adaptability and distract from their core merchant enablement mission. Rather than protect past investments, they committed to change, prioritizing their ability to shift at speed.

Culturally, Shopify reinforced execution speed and adaptability through internal initiatives like Shopify Magic – an AI suite designed not merely to optimize internal efficiency but to enable merchants themselves to respond faster to demand shifts. Leadership success at Shopify is not measured by pipeline reports or internal KPIs alone. It is measured by the speed and effectiveness with which the organization adapts to market opportunities.

Shopify's leadership did not attempt to predict and control future conditions. They built a company structurally and culturally designed to thrive as those conditions changed. In doing so, they operationalized antifragility: creating a system that gains strength, speed, and market position precisely because it is designed to adapt faster than competitors.

## What can we learn?

Leadership reflex is the decisive factor separating companies that adapt from those that decay. Structure enables the possibility of speed. Culture encourages the willingness to move. But only leadership reflex – speed in decision and action at the moments of uncertainty – determines whether the organization adapts in time.

- SAP recognized the shift but delayed action and paid the price.

- Shopify anticipated volatility and built systems that moved faster because of it.

In MLG, the companies that survive will not be those with the best historical advantages. They will be those with leaders willing to dismantle the past and move into the future faster than the market finishes shifting.

## Section 4: The new philosophy of talent

Leadership in MLG companies has two visible jobs: designing structure; and shaping culture. But there is a third, less often acknowledged, that is just as critical – and arguably more difficult. Leaders must select and develop the right people.

However fast and adaptive a leadership team may be, they cannot personally drive every decision or act in every moment of uncertainty. They must build an organization composed of individuals capable of sensing, deciding, and acting at market speed without supervision.

The company's reflexes, ultimately, are built from the reflexes of its people. In MLG, the companies that survive will not be those with the best historical advantages. They will be those whose leaders have built organizations full of individuals willing and able to move into the future faster, adapting in real time as the market shifts.

### From specialists to adaptive generalists

Traditional hiring prioritized specialists: individuals who could execute a narrow function inside a stable environment. In MLG companies, specialization without adaptability becomes a liability. Market conditions shift faster than static roles evolve. Skills that were critical 12 months ago may be obsolete today. Adaptive generalists – individuals capable of mastering multiple disciplines, integrating knowledge across domains, and flexing into new roles as business needs change – become the foundation of organizational reflex.

The goal is not to hire for breadth at the expense of depth. It is to hire individuals who have a level of depth in one area and then use that to think laterally into other problem sets. It's not depth for its own sake, but depth *so it can be used elsewhere.* Portability becomes mandatory.

## From corporate ladders to talent marketplaces

In companies built for stable markets, career progression followed predictable ladders. Tenure and title dictated access to opportunity and influence. MLG companies replace this model with internal talent marketplaces: dynamic systems where movement across teams, projects, and domains is driven by business need and demonstrated capability.

The highest-leverage employees are not those who ascend titles predictably. They are those who move to where the company's steepest learning curves and most critical challenges emerge. Leadership must create environments where this movement is expected and rewarded, not treated as deviation from the norm.

## From static job descriptions to dynamic value creation

Job descriptions, static documents outlining predefined responsibilities, assume a static environment. In MLG companies, the relevance of a role shifts faster than a document can be updated. Execution is judged not by adherence to a list, but by the ability to solve real problems under changing conditions.

Hiring and performance evaluation must focus on the ability to deliver outcomes, adapt to new demands, and solve emerging customer needs – not on checklist compliance. In adaptive companies, employees are measured by the value they create, not adherence to the role they were hired to fill.

## From tenure-based compensation to impact-based rewards

Traditional compensation systems reward longevity. Time served becomes a proxy for contribution. In MLG organizations, that logic fails. Contribution must be measured in terms of learning velocity, execution speed, and market impact – not the passage of time.

High performers in an adaptive system do not wait for annual reviews to be recognized. They are rewarded based on the velocity and magnitude of the value they create. Incentive structures must reinforce execution speed, adaptability, and problem-solving under uncertainty, or they will reinforce inertia instead.

## Leadership's responsibility: Hiring for learning velocity

Talent strategy cannot be delegated to HR departments operating under outdated assumptions. Hiring is a core leadership discipline. In MLG, the relevant question is not 'Has this person done the job before?' but 'Can this person figure out what needs to be done next?'

Adaptive companies hire individuals capable of disconfirming their own assumptions, operating effectively under ambiguity, and building new approaches when the old ones collapse. Past success is a data point, not a guarantee. The only defensible hiring bet is on learning velocity and execution initiative.

Leadership is ultimately responsible for whether the organization's reflexes strengthen or decay at the edge. Without people who embody adaptability at a personal level, structural decentralization and cultural reinforcement will collapse under pressure.

## Conclusion: Leaders as system architects of MLG

Leadership in MLG organizations is not about commanding plans from the center. It is about designing systems that adapt continuously at the edge. Structure, culture, and people are the critical components of that system. Without a structure built for decentralized decision-making, an organization cannot move fast enough. Without a culture that rewards speed, learning, and iteration, the structure decays into inertia. Without people capable of sensing and acting under ambiguity, even the best-designed systems will fail to adapt in real time.

Leadership reflex is expressed not just in decisions made, but in the systems built – the operating models, the norms, and the talent selected to reinforce adaptability. Leaders are not just responsible for setting direction. They are responsible for ensuring that every part of the company, from executive team to market pod, can move as fast as the conditions around them change.

But leadership systems cannot be left to intuition. MLG organizations also need to measure the reflexes they have built. They must track whether the organization is learning as fast, executing as fast, and adapting as fast as the market demands.

In the next chapter, we will define the metrics that allow leaders to manage MLG as a system – providing early signals of strength, slippage, and systemic risk before those weaknesses are visible in revenue numbers or market share losses – as well as those metrics that give leaders the lens to grow and maintain those reflexes themselves.

# 8

# The metrics that matter in Market-Led Growth

## Introduction: The diagnostic dashboard

Leadership in a Market-Led Growth (MLG) company is not just about direction – it's about building a system that can sense, decide, and adapt faster than the market moves. That system cannot be managed by instinct alone. It requires comparable measurement (yes, the ghost of Peter Drucker is with you). You need to know where the reflexes are working – and where they're beginning to decay – before the damage shows up in revenue or retention curves.

In high-change markets, you need *leading indicators* – metrics that expose early signs of strategic decay before they become visible in outcomes. They are not artifacts of bureaucratic reporting. They are the company's diagnostic tools – showing where the system is learning, where it's stuck, and where alignment is starting to drift. In an MLG company, leadership does not rely on overly-weighted executive anecdote, quarterly review meetings, or lagging financial KPIs to evaluate performance. It manages through continuous feedback loops – real-time indicators of adaptive health across pods, teams, and motions.

Metrics do two things in an MLG system. First, they reinforce *structural focus*. They help leaders and operators see where execution is succeeding or stalling across the business – not just in output, but in responsiveness. They show whether pods are aligned to signal, whether learning is compounding, and whether scale is happening with control or without it.

Second, they reinforce *cultural discipline*. MLG companies don't celebrate experimentation for its own sake. They value experiments that generate useful signal and drive iteration. Metrics surface the difference. They expose when learning has become ritual – testing for testing's sake – and when it's still a live mechanism for improving fit.

> This is not a rejection of traditional financial metrics. Revenue growth, margin expansion, customer acquisition costs (CAC), Pipeline, net retained revenue (NRR), etc. – all of these still matter. They remain the essential scorecard for the business. But they are *lagging indicators*. By the time they reveal a problem, the window for competitive response may have already closed.

In this chapter, we'll define four core metrics that serve as early-warning signals for reflex health. Each tracks a different dimension of adaptability:

1. **Revenue per market pod (RPP)** – Measures the financial productivity of each pod, ensuring accountability at the edge.
2. **Magic number per pod** – Tracks sales efficiency to prevent premature scaling before fit is proven.
3. **Failure yield ratio (FYR)** – Measures whether failed initiatives generate useful signal and rapid iteration.
4. **Market activation speed (MAS)** – Captures how quickly the company senses a market shift, learns from it, and acts.

These metrics don't replace traditional dashboards. They sit underneath them – instrumenting the system that produces growth, before growth becomes visible. This chapter is about how to build and use them well. Forgive me – in this chapter, there's a fair bit of example, and even an equation or two – but indulge me, the metrics are important.

## Metric 1: Revenue per market pod (RPP)

This is about ensuring financial accountability at the execution level. Most traditional companies measure revenue at a broad, company-wide level, assessing growth in sweeping financial statements that aggregate performance across multiple teams, initiatives, and geographies. This approach creates blind spots. It hides inefficiencies and allows underperforming teams to continue operating simply because they are buried within an overall revenue target. MLG companies take a different approach. They measure revenue at the *pod level*, ensuring that every market team operates with real-time financial accountability.

By tracking revenue on a per-pod basis, companies can identify which market teams are delivering real traction and which are burning resources without results. This creates a clear feedback loop: when a pod proves its ability to generate revenue efficiently, it receives *more investment, faster* – without waiting for an annual budget cycle.

Conversely, if a pod struggles to demonstrate traction, leadership can intervene early and either refocus its approach or redirect resources elsewhere. In an MLG model, financial accountability is not just a corporate reporting requirement – it is the mechanism that keeps teams aligned and ensures that *capital follows performance, not assumptions*.

## Metric 2: Magic number per pod

For years, go-to-market (GTM) leaders have relied on the *magic number* – a calculation that compares new revenue to GTM costs to determine efficiency. You simply divide new revenue in a time period by the cost of your GTM function (sales, marketing, and so on) in that period. It remains a valuable concept, but in MLG, it must be applied at the pod level rather than being treated as a single, company-wide ratio. MLG organizations cannot afford to scale based on broad financial trends; they must scale based on real-time traction.

Tracking the magic number at the pod level ensures that no GTM motion scales prematurely. A market pod that delivers strong revenue growth relative to investment can receive more funding to accelerate expansion. A pod that struggles to generate returns, however, cannot hide behind an overall company-wide efficiency score. This approach forces market teams to demonstrate that their motions are working before additional resources are committed.

By treating efficiency as a function of real-time execution rather than a historical financial benchmark, MLG companies ensure that capital allocation remains a living process, not a static plan.

## Metric 3: Failure yield ratio (FYR)

Traditional organizations often view failure as wasted effort. In an MLG company, failure is not the problem – failure without learning is the problem. Underperforming pods – *what isn't working* – is as useful as what is working, if you're moving and learning at speed. The failure yield ratio (FYR) is a fundamental execution metric that measures how effectively teams turn failed experiments into valuable insights.

The concept behind FYR is simple: an experiment is only valuable if it generates useful knowledge that leads to better execution. If a test fails but provides clear insights that can be acted upon quickly, it has contributed to the company's learning velocity. If a test fails and no actionable insights emerge – or if insights are discovered but never implemented – then that experiment was a wasted effort. It encourages teams to *maximize learnings, act fast, and optimize spend* – all critical for MLG.

By tracking FYR over time, leadership can identify which pods are learning efficiently and which are simply *running experiments for the sake of experimentation*. If a pod has a high FYR, it signals that the team is continuously refining its approach and applying what it learns at speed. If a pod's FYR is low, it may indicate that the team is either failing to extract insights from its tests or is too slow in turning those insights into execution.

Unlike traditional success metrics, which often focus solely on outcomes, *FYR rewards the process of rapid iteration*. It recognizes that in a fast-moving market, the best companies are not the ones that avoid failure – they are the ones that *fail well and use those failures to improve faster than the competition*.

The formula:

> **FYR = (Number of Learnings × Speed of Implementation) / Cost of Experiment** (in thousands of dollars)

- **Number of learnings**: Each unique insight extracted from an experiment counts as **one learning**.
  - Example: Discovering that **Reddit converts better than Google** → 1 learning
  - Learning that **women engage more than men AND that their primary concern is safety** → 2 learnings
- **Speed of implementation**: The faster an insight can be acted upon, the higher its value.
  - 3 = Today
  - 2 = Within a week
  - 1 = More than a week
  - 0 = Never (**the learning was interesting but not actionable yet**)
  - If multiple learnings have different lead times, take the **average speed of implementation**.
- **Cost of experiment**: The total financial cost, measured in thousands of dollars.

## Pod-level FYR formula

> **Pod Average FYR = (Σ FYR of all experiments in a given period) / Total number of experiments in that period**

- **Higher pod-level FYR** → Teams are learning fast and implementing insights efficiently.
- **Lower pod-level FYR** → Experiments may be too expensive, slow, or yielding too few insights.

Pods should be partially judged and incentivized based on their average FYR over time, fostering a culture of constant learning and rapid iteration. Organizations can compare FYRs across pods to see which teams are best at running efficient experiments, where learning velocity is the highest, and if some pods are acting too slowly or spending inefficiently. It's crucial that FYR shouldn't be used as a weapon – the goal is to continuously improve, not punish. The key is to help pods benchmark themselves, optimize experiments, and refine execution speed.

## Key considerations for applying failure yield ratio (FYR)

*No single FYR score defines success or failure universally.* What constitutes a strong or weak FYR is highly dependent on the company's business model, deal size, and cost structure. A software-as-a-service (SaaS) business charging US$50 per month for its product must be far more judicious about experimentation costs than a company selling US$1M enterprise deals. In one case, a US$50,000 test would represent an enormous investment relative to revenue, while in the other, it may be an insignificant cost of doing business.

*The right way to use FYR is not to fixate on an absolute benchmark*, but to evaluate experiments in the context of historical company data. Leadership should track FYR over time, identify trends, and flag anything that deviates from established norms. If a company's typical experiments yield an FYR of 0.6, and a new set of tests suddenly drop to 0.2, it's a sign to investigate. The goal is not to meet an arbitrary threshold but to ensure that experimentation is becoming more efficient over time.

When it comes to how learnings are valued, MLG takes a fundamentally different approach from traditional success metrics. In many organizations, only 'big' insights are celebrated – the transformative discoveries that change an entire GTM strategy or open up a new market. But in reality, you don't always know in the moment which insight will be the breakthrough. Sometimes, what seems like a minor learning at first – a slight shift in messaging, a new customer segment behaving unexpectedly – becomes the insight that cascades into a major strategic shift.

*Because of this uncertainty, the FYR model weights all learnings equally.* Instead of attempting to rank the perceived value of each insight, the focus is on maximizing overall learning velocity – ensuring that teams are extracting as many actionable insights as possible in each cycle of experimentation.

Speed is another critical factor that distinguishes FYR from traditional success metrics. In MLG, speed is not just an operational advantage – it is the advantage. The companies that iterate and implement learnings faster than the competition win the market. That's why the FYR model deliberately *penalizes experiments that take too long to implement*. If a team extracts an insight but sits on it for weeks before taking action, the window of opportunity may have already closed. To reflect this urgency, any insight that takes more than a week to implement is automatically devalued in the model. If an experiment produces multiple insights with different lead times, the FYR calculation uses the average speed of implementation, ensuring that execution velocity remains at the core of the metric.

Ultimately, FYR is not about rewarding failure – it is about ensuring that every failure is understood as what it really is – learning. Companies that apply this metric well will find themselves learning faster, executing smarter, and adapting ahead of the competition.

*Examples of FYR in action*

## Example 1: Running shoe brand testing market positioning

A sneaker brand spends **US$30,000** on a paid search experiment across **Google**, **TikTok**, and **Reddit**, testing messaging around comfort, safety, and distance running.

### Results:

1. **Long-distance messaging** has no traction across any platform → 1 learning
2. **Mid-distance messaging** performs **great on Reddit** but poorly elsewhere → 1 learning
3. **Comfort resonates on TikTok and Google, but not Reddit** → 1 learning
4. **Safety messaging works only on TikTok, with women engaging most** → 1 learning
5. **Immediate response: they adjust their ad spend accordingly** → 1 learning

### FYR calculation:

- **Learnings = 5**
- **Speed of implementation = 4 out of 5 can be implemented today** → **Average speed = 3**
- **Cost** = US$30,000 → **30 in thousands**

FYR = 5 × 330 = 0.5 FYR = 305 × 3 = **0.5**

**Interpretation:** A strong experiment – **high learnings, fast execution, and reasonable cost**.

## Example 2: Sneaker brand testing influencer marketing

A sneaker company spends **US$10,000** hiring a research firm to identify which influencers resonate most with their audience.

### Results:

1. They get a list of **25 influencers**, but most are **high-cost celebrities** → 1 learning
2. They find **young men prefer mainstream athletes, while young women follow online influencers** → 1 learning
3. They must **negotiate contracts, delaying implementation for weeks** → Speed = 1

### FYR calculation:

- **Learnings = 2**
- **Speed of implementation = 1**
- **Cost = US$10,000 → 10 in thousands**

**FYR = 2 × 110 = 0.2 FYR = 102 × 1 =0.2**

**Interpretation: Low FYR** – costly and slow, with limited actionable insights.

### What's a good FYR?

There's **no universal 'good' FYR** – it depends on your business. Instead of using a fixed threshold, track FYR **over time** and compare against **your company's historical average**:

- **Above average** FYR → Invest more in similar experiments
- **Below average** FYR → Identify **why** (too few learnings, slow implementation, high cost)

If an FYR is outside your standard deviation, dig deeper. This is an innovation plus velocity metric that deliberately rewards high-learning experiments.

- **Speed matters** – slow implementation **lowers** an experiment's FYR
- **Track your own trends** – acceptable FYR **varies by business model**
- Use FYR as **a diagnostic tool**, not a rigid pass/fail test

## Metric 4: Market activation speed (MAS)

In an MLG environment, success is rarely determined by who has the best idea. More often, it is dictated by who can execute the fastest. Market shifts rarely go unnoticed – competitors, customers, and analysts often spot the same trends at roughly the same time. But while some companies act immediately, adjusting their strategy and capitalizing on the change, others become trapped in their own internal machinery – bogged down by endless approvals, strategic hesitations, and the inertia of established processes.

Market activation speed (MAS) ensures that a company's reflexes match the speed of the market. It measures how quickly an organization learns something and turns that insight into a market-facing change, relative to the scale of the change itself. The bigger the transformation, the more moving parts are affected – but MAS ensures that even large shifts happen at a competitive speed.

MAS is calculated as:

> **Size of change / time elapsed (in days) from internal learning to market execution**

Where the **size of the change** is determined by the number of parts of the organization that must adjust how they operate:

- **10** → Minor tweaks that impact a single function, such as updating ad copy in a campaign.
- **6** → A significant shift affecting two or more teams, such as changing messaging for an ideal customer profile (ICP) within a market (impacting both marketing and sales).
- **4** → A major shift requiring coordination across four or more functions, such as a fundamental product repositioning that alters GTM strategy, pricing, and customer messaging.
- **1** → A **huge structural change** that impacts a majority of the business, such as moving from subscription-based pricing to usage-based pricing – which requires changes across marketing, sales, finance, engineering, and customer support.

A **low MAS** indicates a company is still operating at an **internal pace**, adjusting strategy in slow-moving cycles dictated by planning meetings and leadership approvals rather than real-time market feedback.

A **high MAS**, on the other hand, signals an organization that is **adapting at market speed**, adjusting execution the moment an insight becomes clear and capturing opportunities before competitors have even started their internal discussions.

## MAS in action: The difference between high and low market activation speed

The true power of MAS becomes clear when you compare how different companies respond to the same type of market shift. A company with high MAS rapidly learns, adapts, and executes, gaining a competitive edge before rivals even begin their strategic discussions. A company with low MAS, on the other hand, gets caught in its own internal inertia, allowing the market to shift while it lags behind.

## Example 1: High MAS – a streaming service adapts to AI-generated content

A major streaming platform detects a spike in consumer interest in AI-generated content after an independent creator releases an AI-powered animated series that goes viral. The data team flags this trend in real time, noting increased engagement across social platforms and a 30% rise in searches related to AI-generated movies.

Within four days, the content acquisition team secures licensing deals with emerging AI-generated content creators, and the marketing team launches a new category page promoting AI-powered films. By the end of the second week, the product team updates the recommendation algorithm to highlight AI-generated content for users who have engaged with similar media.

Even though this wasn't part of the company's original content roadmap, their ability to detect the shift and act immediately gives them a first-mover advantage. Competitors, still locked in quarterly planning cycles, take months to approve similar initiatives, by which time the trend has matured and early adopters have already been captured.

**MAS score calculation:**

- **Size of change:** 6 (Cross-functional impact: marketing, content acquisition, product, and data teams all had to adjust)
- **Time elapsed:** 10 days

**MAS = 6 days / 10 days = 0.6**

This high MAS score reflects the company's ability to react within days, not months, allowing it to capitalize on the AI-generated content wave before it became mainstream.

## Example 2: Low MAS – an enterprise SaaS company struggles to adjust pricing strategy

An enterprise SaaS company notices a drop in win rates among mid-market customers after a competitor introduces a usage-based pricing model. The sales team flags this shift, reporting that prospects are increasingly pushing back on the company's rigid subscription pricing.

The pricing team gathers data, confirming that 40% of lost deals cite pricing inflexibility as a key reason for choosing a competitor. However, rather than responding immediately, the company falls into a cycle of internal discussions and leadership approvals.

First, a three-week analysis is conducted to model potential revenue impact. Then, the finance and product teams conduct another month-long review to explore implementation feasibility. After that, the leadership team debates for another six weeks whether they should launch a limited pilot or a full rollout.

By the time they introduce a usage-based option four months later, the competitive landscape has shifted even further. The competitor, already winning deals with its pricing flexibility, has since refined its approach, iterating based on live customer feedback. Meanwhile, the SaaS company is still in the process of training its sales team on how to sell the new model.

## MAS score calculation:

- **Size of change:** 1 (pricing strategy overhaul affects the entire business: finance, sales, marketing, engineering, and customer support)
- **Time elapsed:** 120 days

## MAS = 1 day / 120 days = 0.008

This MAS score signals a company that, despite recognizing a market shift early, allowed internal processes to slow execution. The delay cost them months of lost deals and forced them into a defensive position, while their competitor continued to iterate and widen the gap.

## Why MAS balances both speed and scale

The purpose of MAS isn't to favor small, quick changes over big, important ones – or vice versa. Instead, it weighs the significance of a change against the time it takes to implement.

A small tweak – such as adjusting ad messaging – should be implemented almost instantly. The longer it takes, the lower its MAS score and the clearer it becomes that execution bottlenecks are at play. Conversely, large-scale transformations will naturally take longer, but they still need to happen with urgency. A company cannot justify taking six months to implement a strategic pricing shift just because it's complex.

This balance ensures that MAS does not allow complexity to become an excuse for slowness. Just because a change is large does not mean it can be stretched across an entire quarter. A low MAS is a warning sign – a signal that the company is either being slowed down by excessive decision-making layers or is unwilling to push through change at a competitive pace.

## Tracking MAS to remove execution bottlenecks

For leadership, tracking MAS forces an honest look at what is slowing execution down. A lagging MAS score often reveals structural inefficiencies: unnecessary approval layers, bloated decision-making processes, or a lack of cross-functional coordination.

If a company consistently struggles to move from insight to execution, leaders must identify whether the issue lies in culture, structure, or incentives. Are teams waiting too long for executive buy-in? Are different functions operating in silos, failing to align quickly on necessary changes? Are there processes designed for stability rather than adaptability?

Addressing these barriers is not about encouraging reckless speed – it is about ensuring that when the market shifts, the organization's ability to react is dictated by opportunity, not bureaucracy.

At its core, MAS is about removing excuses for slowness. If your company can identify a necessary change, it should be able to make that change before the market moves past it. The faster an organization can act on what it learns, the more it dictates the terms of competition – forcing others to react instead of playing catch-up itself.

## Why these four metrics keep MLG companies aligned

Together, RPP, magic number, FYR, and MAS create a framework for execution that prioritizes real-time adaptability over static planning. They shift leadership's focus away from backward-looking efficiency metrics and toward forward-looking indicators of speed, agility, and learning velocity.

Revenue per market pod ensures that every team is financially accountable, preventing wasted investment in unproductive motions. Magic number ensures that growth scales based on actual traction, not assumptions. FYR guarantees that every experiment contributes to the company's learning velocity. MAS ensures that execution happens at market speed, not corporate speed.

For MLG leaders, these four metrics serve as the pulse of adaptive execution. They don't just track whether teams are working hard or making progress; they measure whether teams are moving in the right direction at the right speed. In a market where adaptability determines success, that distinction is everything.

Metrics, however, only expose where action is needed; they do not make the decisions. MLG companies must respond to the signals with decisive, dynamic movement – realigning resources continuously to match live market realities. This is a job that everyone in the company is part of, in one way or another. In MLG, resource allocation is not a static financial plan locked in by quarterly or annual cycles. It is an adaptive muscle, integrated into the system of continuous sensing, deciding, and acting.

# 9

# Adaptive capital and planning

## Introduction: Capital speed is company speed

Imagine this: a pod notices an unexpected spike in engagement from a new buyer persona. They tweak the messaging, reposition the offer, and get early signal: higher click-through rates, warmer discovery calls, faster qualification. The pod flags the opportunity, but they've already exhausted their discretionary budget for the quarter.

Additional headcount has been frozen since the last planning cycle. The specialists they need – data science, legal, pricing – are tied up on previously funded priorities. Leadership is supportive, but there's no clear path to reallocate resources until Q3. The moment starts to fade. This is not a failure of insight, it's a failure of planning and capital allocation structures.

Every company wants to be adaptive. It wants to move with the market, adjust to new information, and respond quickly to customer needs. But in practice, most organizations are only as adaptive as their resourcing systems allow. A team may spot early traction. A pod may uncover signal. But if capital can't move – and if people can't be reassigned – then nothing will happen.

What gets funded is what gets built. What gets staffed is what gets sold. A company can't execute faster than it can reallocate, and that's where many systems break – not at the level of strategy, or even execution – but at the point where resources are supposed to follow reality. This is the hidden constraint behind most go-to-market (GTM) lag. Teams know what to do, but can't move the money, shift the headcount, or unlock the dependencies. Budgets are locked, plans are fixed, and roles are tethered to past decisions. The result is drift: not because the market changed, but because the company couldn't.

Market-Led Growth (MLG) depends on responsiveness – on a company's ability to align what it does with what the market is telling it. But responsiveness isn't just cultural, it's operational. It shows up in how capital flows and how resourcing decisions get made. If those systems are slow, everything else becomes performative.

This chapter is about fixing the bottleneck. It's about rethinking how resources move – money, people, and permission – and building the infrastructure to support fluid, signal-driven allocation. That means changing how you plan. It means treating capital as a living system, and it means shifting the company's mental model from resourcing as commitment to *resourcing as adaptation*.

## Planning and capital: Two systems, one problem

Every company has a version of the annual planning cycle. It starts with forecasts, cascades through headcount and budget requests, and resolves into a detailed picture of the year ahead: what will be funded, who will be hired, which priorities will be staffed. On paper, it looks like alignment. In reality, it often functions more like a temporary truce – an agreement between teams based on negotiated assumptions that rarely survive first contact with the market.

Once the plan is locked, it starts driving behavior. Budgets become fixed, hiring decisions get frozen in place, program timelines are set, and even when the plan starts to age – as segments shift, signal emerges, or early bets stall – the system is slow to adjust. Changes require escalation. Reallocation is seen as failure. Everyone knows conditions have changed, but no one wants to be the first to admit that the plan no longer fits.

This is where capital allocation enters the picture – not as a separate issue, but as the enforcement mechanism of the plan. Budgeting formalizes what planning assumes. It sets resources in motion, locks spending into categories, and binds teams to decisions made months earlier under different conditions. If planning imagines the future, capital makes it real – and rigid.

That's the structural problem. Planning and capital are treated as two systems, but they're really two sides of the same constraint. Together, they create the illusion of control while embedding organizational lag. One locks assumptions into priorities. The other locks those priorities into funding. By the time the market moves, the company is already committed somewhere else.

MLG challenges this cycle directly. It doesn't discard planning or abandon budgeting, instead, it retools both to serve adaptation. Planning becomes a way to identify high-variance bets, not to pretend at certainty. Budgeting becomes a mechanism for fluid investment, not fixed entitlement. Not every dollar must be spent at once – or even apportioned to quarter, or even year, and both systems are redesigned to treat movement – not stability – as the normal state.

What emerges is a single principle: *resources must follow signal*. If the company sees traction, the system should shift toward it. If a bet loses momentum, the system should redirect. That doesn't mean constant churn, it means continuous realignment. The plan is still valuable, but it's only as good as the company's ability to revise it at speed.

## Principles of adaptive capital allocation

If the traditional model treats capital as part of a plan to be executed, MLG treats it as a portfolio to be adjusted. The difference is not just philosophical. In a dynamic system, capital needs to move at the speed of signal. That requires a different logic. Not looser governance, but smarter mechanisms. Not abandoning discipline, but applying it differently.

Here are four principles that define adaptive capital.

## 1. Money follows momentum

In most organizations, funding flows toward size. Mature business lines, large regions, or well-resourced teams tend to attract more budget – because they're established, visible, and often better at advocating for themselves. But momentum doesn't always live where scale does.

Adaptive capital flips the lens. It asks: Where is traction building? Which pods are learning fastest? Where is early signal emerging – before it's mature enough to look impressive in a board deck? In this model, capital isn't used to reinforce what's already proven. It's used to accelerate what's just starting to work.

This isn't gambling, but disciplined bias. A pod that moves quickly, generates clear signal, and demonstrates pattern recognition should be able to pull capital – not wait for it. If momentum can't attract resources, the system is structurally slow.

## 2. Cut fast, fund fast

In many companies, once budget is assigned, it stays where it is – even if the original rationale erodes. Teams hang on to underperforming spend because returning it feels like an admission of failure. Leadership is slow to intervene for fear of sending the wrong message, and the budget becomes sticky.

That stickiness is toxic. Capital must be reallocated not just when things collapse, but when signal softens. Pulling back funding must become culturally normalized. It's not a punishment, it's hygiene. Likewise, injecting new capital into a pod that's outperforming can't wait for the next planning cycle. It needs to happen in rhythm with reality.

Cut fast, fund fast – both are signs of a system running optimally.

## 3. Preserve optionality

Traditional budgeting rewards certainty. Teams that show confidence, long-range projections, and clean plans often win the allocation conversation. But long-range certainty, in a high-change environment, is often an illusion.

MLG budgets for optionality. That means not spending every dollar up front. It means keeping some percentage of capital and headcount in strategic reserve – not for emergencies, but for signal-responsive moves. It means building budget structures that can flex: fewer hard-coded line items, more modular buckets that allow local interpretation.

Optionality isn't waste, it's the precondition for agility.

## 4. Allocation is a collaboration

In many organizations, budget decisions are a contest. Teams lobby, posture, and defend. Finance plays the referee. The result is political capital allocation – driven as much by narrative strength as by signal strength.

Adaptive capital reframes the relationship. Finance becomes a partner in pattern recognition. Strategic leads, pod owners, and finance analysts collaborate to interpret signal, test hypotheses, and co-design resource flows. The best questions aren't 'What do you need?' or 'What can you justify?' they're 'What are we seeing?' and 'Where should we lean in?'

This isn't about being nice, it's about replacing competition with coordination – so that capital flows where learning is happening, not just where influence sits. This is one of the reasons why culture and structure are so important – and why failure must be seen as *learning* in an MLG model.

A framing of 'failing' pods will ultimately reduce back to a defensive fight for resources. But pods that are 'learning' can always add value.

It's also about decoupling 'people' from the 'pod' – you might decide to call time on a pod, but that doesn't mean the team lose their jobs – they can be re-allocated and start learning in a new one.

Taken together, these principles make resourcing a live system. Not a fixed commitment, not a quarterly negotiation, but a continuous mechanism for adapting to reality. When teams see momentum, they can act. When conditions change, the system adjusts. That's not chaos, that's what responsiveness looks like at scale.

## Structural enablers

Adaptive capital isn't a posture, it's a system. Without real infrastructure, the most well-intentioned talk of flexibility and responsiveness turns into empty rhetoric. Leaders say they want to reallocate fast – but the budget model doesn't support it. Pods are encouraged to move on signal – but there's no path to unlock cross-functional support. Finance wants to be a partner – but the tooling reinforces static controls.

If you want resources to move with signal, the system has to allow for that movement. That means building structural mechanisms that support reallocation – at the level of money, headcount, and access. In MLG, that infrastructure doesn't sit in theory, it shows up in five operational shifts.

### 1. Live investment portfolios

Most companies track performance, not optionality. They look at revenue, pipeline, burn. But they don't maintain a live view of how capital is distributed across pods or initiatives – and what that distribution says about responsiveness.

MLG companies treat investments like a living portfolio. They track where money is going, how each pod is performing (using shared metrics like market activation speed (MAS) or revenue per market pod (RPP)), and whether capital is concentrated in high-signal areas – or still tied to historical priorities. This portfolio view doesn't replace

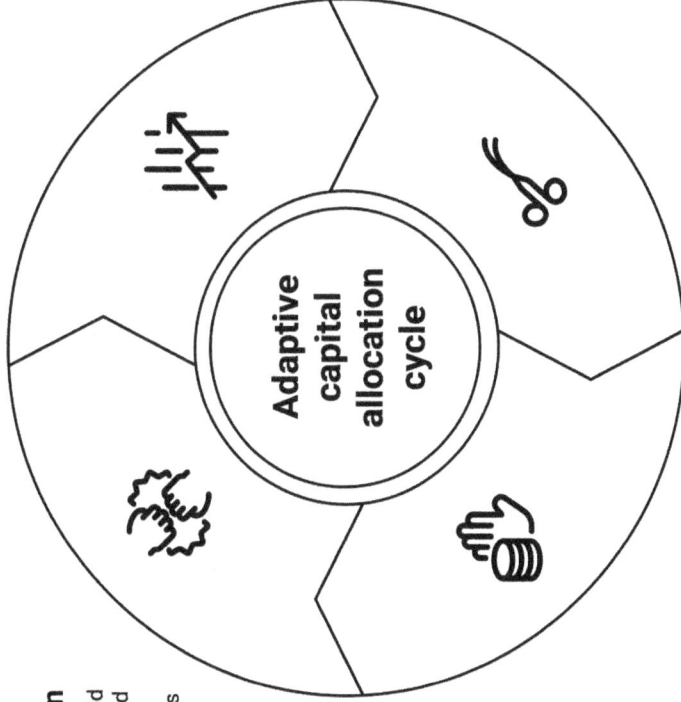

**Follow momentum**

Capital should flow to where traction is emerging, even if it's early. Don't just fund what's already scaled, but accelerate what's starting to break through.

**Cut fast, fund fast**

When something's not working, pull the plug quickly. When a pod is performing, back it immediately. Speed in both directions is what keeps the system responsive.

**Collaborative allocation**

Finance and pod leaders should make decisions together, based on real-time patterns and not politics, posturing, or last year's assumptions.

**Preserve optionality**

Don't spend every dollar up front. Keep some capital in reserve so you can act fast when new signals appear or priorities shift.

**Figure 19** In MLG, capital is alive, it flows to learning, not lobbying – cut fast, fund fast, and keep optionality open. Momentum, not maturity, drives investment.

financial discipline, it sharpens it. The question isn't just: 'How are we spending?' it's, 'Are we still investing in the right things and in the right way with the right outcomes?'

## 2.  Flexible budget models

In a traditional system, budgets are approved by line item. Spend is locked to categories: events, tools, contractors, campaigns. Any change requires justification, escalation, and reapproval. The result is friction. Teams either overspend to make use of the budget, or underspend and risk losing it next cycle.

An adaptive budget model looks different. It emphasizes flexibility over granularity. Budgets might be structured into larger, intent-based pools – discovery, growth, retention, GTM experiments – rather than hard-coded categories. Reallocation within a pod is expected. Reallocation across pods is facilitated by a small number of centrally managed reserves, which can be deployed based on signal.

## 3.  Modular headcount

Headcount is often treated as the most fixed resource. Once a role is approved, it belongs to a team – even if the need changes. But in MLG, where opportunity shifts quickly, treating headcount as static creates organizational lag.

Instead, roles can be modular. A portion of headcount is reserved for high-signal redeployment: specialist roles that 'float' across pods, unassigned FTEs that can be activated mid-quarter, or short-term allocations of shared services (data, legal, security) that follow momentum. Some companies manage this through internal marketplaces or resourcing councils. Others do it informally. Either way, the logic is the same: staff follows signal – not just strategy.

## 4. Ongoing investment reviews

Annual planning is too slow. Quarterly reviews are often too detached. To stay responsive, resourcing decisions need a tighter rhythm.

MLG companies run monthly (or biweekly) investment reviews – not as performance rituals, but as part of signal interpretation sessions. Pod leaders, finance, and leadership come together to ask: What's moving? What's losing traction? What bets are becoming clearer? These aren't multi-hour judgment sessions. They're fast reallocation mechanisms. Sometimes the answer is to stay the course. Sometimes it's to cut, reinvest, or shift direction. The point is not to be reactive, it's to spot emerging opportunities and sharpen focus on existing ones, as well as *stop* those that were a false promise or are fading away.

## 5. Shared dashboards, shared language

None of this works without shared understanding. Pods can't ask for support if they can't contextualize their progress. Finance can't partner effectively if it's operating on a different timescale or metric set. Leadership can't prioritize if it doesn't see the pattern.

That's why adaptive capital relies on shared metrics – not for performance grading, but for pattern recognition. Metrics like MAS, RPP, and failure yield ratio (FYR), alongside the standard metrics, help ground decisions in common frames of reference. Everyone sees the same thing. Everyone knows how to talk about it. That reduces negotiation friction and increases the speed of agreement.

Adaptation isn't just about loosening the reins, it's about building systems that allow change to happen deliberately, repeatedly, and without creating chaos. These structural enablers aren't 'nice to have' upgrades. They're prerequisites for any company that wants its capital to move at the speed of its market.

## Leadership's job is resource stewardship

In most companies, leadership's role in resourcing is episodic. They set the plan, approve the budget, weigh in on escalations, and occasionally step in to resolve conflicts. These decisions are positioned as moments of judgment – allocations of trust, signals of confidence, rewards for performance – and because they are episodic, they carry weight. The result is a system where resource movements are seen as status signals – where gaining budget is winning, and giving it up is losing.

In an adaptive system, this logic doesn't hold. Resource shifts happen regularly. Capital moves as signal moves. Some initiatives gain ground, others lose it. If every reallocation is treated as a reputational event, the system becomes paralyzed. No one wants to give budget back, teams hide drift, leaders hold on to stale bets, and the entire structure tilts toward inertia.

So, in MLG, leadership must take on a different role: not the approver of requests, but the steward of capital flow. That means designing a system where movement is normal, where giving back resources is treated as hygiene, not failure, and where asking for more – when signal supports it – is a sign of clarity, not arrogance.

This requires both structural changes and cultural ones. Structurally, leaders must build the mechanisms: flexible budgeting, reserve capital, signal-led reviews, modular headcount. But culturally, they must model the behavior. That means:

- Rewarding teams that proactively reallocate away from underperforming bets.
- Publicly supporting resource moves that follow signal, even when politically inconvenient.
- Framing resource shifts as a feature of a working system – not an exception, and certainly not a crisis.

Leaders also need to abandon the illusion that resourcing is ever fully 'solved.' In adaptive systems, resourcing is never done, it's a continuous function. The role of leadership is not to fix allocation once, but to keep it in motion – deliberately, clearly, and in alignment with the company's strategic intent.

The question isn't whether every resourcing decision will be right. It's whether the system allows enough movement for the company to course-correct without delay. That's what adaptive leadership looks like: not heroic intervention, but active, consistent stewardship of the system that responds to signal at the edge.

## Culture change is part of the system

You can't change how capital moves without also changing how people feel about capital. In most organizations, resourcing is emotional. Budget is tied to status. Headcount signals trust. Teams protect their allocations not just because they need them – but because giving them up feels like a loss of power, or relevance, or political capital.

This is not a character flaw, it's the natural outcome of systems where resources are hard-won, slow-moving, and inconsistently revisited. When reallocation is rare, it becomes personal. When the only time a team loses funding is during a crisis or performance review, then every shift carries judgment.

MLG requires a different relationship with resources. In an adaptive company, movement is not an exception – it's the norm. Some initiatives gain ground. Others lose it. Momentum changes. Signal emerges. The resourcing system reflects that reality, and the culture makes it safe to work inside it.

That means dismantling some deeply held assumptions:

- That budget is a reward for past success.
- That headcount is a proxy for importance.
- That changing course signals weakness.

And replacing them with new defaults:

- That optionality is strategic.
- That pulling back resources is good hygiene.
- That fast, transparent reallocation is a sign of a mature system, not a volatile one.

This isn't easy, it requires leaders to model detachment from sunk costs, it requires finance teams to act as collaborators, not enforcers, and it requires teams to understand that their value isn't measured by the size of their footprint, but by the clarity of their signal and the strength of their response.

Culture change doesn't come after the system – it runs alongside it. A company that builds adaptive resourcing mechanisms without addressing the underlying psychology will find those mechanisms underused, resisted, or gamed. But when culture and structure align, the shift is profound: resources stop being static symbols of power, and start becoming what they're meant to be – tools to help the company learn, adapt, and grow.

## Worked example: The case of pod X

Imagine you have a successful AI inventory tool used by large U.S. retail chains. Now you're testing whether it can be adapted for mid-sized European retailers – a new market with similar challenges but different constraints. These retailers are cost-sensitive, need simpler deployment, and have leaner teams. To explore the opportunity, your team launches a new market pod, backed by funding for marketing, sales hires, and product development.

But two months in, traction is weak, leads are thin, early users say the product works – but it's overengineered and overpriced for their needs. You built for scale and integration; they want plug-and-play.

In a traditional setup, the default response might be to stick to the plan: double down on marketing, push harder on sales, hope momentum kicks in. But in an MLG system, the response is different. The pod doesn't escalate its bet – it adapts it.

## Reallocate resources without spending more

Rather than pouring more money into underperforming channels, the pod redirects existing budget to deepen its understanding of the segment. It runs interviews and focus groups with retail managers, tightening the messaging around ease, speed, and cost-efficiency. Sales reps originally hired to chase big enterprise deals are reassigned to target mid-market prospects – those with immediate need for lighter, simpler tools.

The aim isn't just to salvage the bet, it's to recalibrate it around real signal. That means shifting from a top-down sales play to one that starts with smaller, faster wins – customers who can serve as early references and feedback loops.

## Learn fast, pivot smart

Instead of assuming product-market fit (PMF), the team runs A/B tests on messaging, onboarding, and pricing. The results are clear: mid-sized retailers want fast setup, intuitive dashboards, and lightweight forecasting. The pod moves quickly to modularize the product – less upfront integration, more out-of-the-box value.

A new insight emerges: the best route to market may not be direct sales at all. Local retail consultants already embedded in the industry offer a faster, warmer path in. The pod experiments with partnerships, leveraging existing trust networks to build traction.

## Adapt within constraints

The team doesn't ask for more capital, it reprioritizes. Engineers are repurposed to simplify the UI and remove friction. Plans to expand the enterprise sales team are paused. Instead, the focus shifts to retraining existing reps to sell the new, slimmer offer. Every change happens within the pod's original budget. No new money, just smarter allocation.

### Continuous evaluation, not quarterly panic

Instead of waiting for quarter-end reviews, the pod runs biweekly check-ins with leadership. If the new approach shows traction – measured in pilot conversions, referral interest, or feedback quality – it gets more oxygen. If not, resources shift again. Maybe toward a different market pod. Maybe to a breakout segment elsewhere – no drama, no sunk-cost fallacy, just responsive capital.

### What success looks like

Four months later, the pod looks different. Marketing spend is down 30% – less mass media, more targeted partnerships. Sales is leaner, smarter, and chasing the right customers. The product is simpler and better aligned with user needs. Revenue isn't soaring yet, but momentum is building in the right direction – and the team knows why. The 'bet' has better odds of success.

Meanwhile, another segment unexpectedly explodes. The pod pivots most of its sales and marketing toward it, leaving a skeleton crew to keep learning about the mid-sized space – no turf wars, no drawn-out debates, just fast, high-signal movement.

### The real lesson

This isn't a failure story or a hero tale, it's a systems story. A pod used its autonomy to course-correct in real time, reallocating capital based on feedback, not faith – no extra funding, no panic, just tight loops of signal and response.

This is how MLG organizations stay ahead. They don't run static plans. They build reflexes – teams that sense what's working, shift fast, and optimize without waiting for permission. The pod isn't a silo where sales fights product and marketing argues budget. It's a unit making integrated, adaptive decisions to serve the market better, faster.

And because capital moves with signal, not hierarchy, the organization avoids one of the biggest killers of growth: spending on ideas that looked good on paper but didn't measure up to reality.

## Conclusion: Capital-market fit

Resources are not neutral, they shape behavior, they harden decisions, they lock in assumptions. If they can't move, the company can't either.

MLG demands that capital – financial, human, and organizational – become responsive. That means rethinking planning not as a tool setting a course, but as a structure for managing change. It means building systems that allow money, people, and attention to follow signal, and it means shifting the culture around resourcing from entitlement to adaptation.

You don't need to plan perfectly, you need to plan for movement, because the real work of building a responsive company isn't just sensing the market – it's backing what you learn.

# 10

# AI-native execution: Enabling Market-Led Growth

## Introduction: AI is not the operating system – MLG is

The operating system of modern growth is Market-Led Growth (MLG). It is a systemic approach to execution: decentralized, signal-driven, and structured for adaptability. Its power lies in its ability to translate live market signals into fast, coordinated action across the organization. But while MLG is the system, it is AI that enables it to run at speed.

Without AI, MLG is possible – but only theoretically. The workflows required to sense, interpret, and respond to market changes continuously can be executed manually. But that is expensive, slow, and difficult to scale. For most companies, the cost of decentralization without automation is prohibitive. Leadership becomes a bottleneck, coordination breaks down, and feedback loops lag behind the market. What AI offers is not just efficiency, it is viability. It makes the MLG model executable in real-time conditions.

### The shift from cost-cutting to strategic enablement

Most companies still treat AI as a tactical tool: a faster spreadsheet, a cheaper analyst, a more scalable content generator. The dominant use case is still the automation of routine work – extracting efficiency from existing processes rather than rethinking the operating model. But this constrains AI to the role of productivity enhancer, rather than strategic enabler. It assumes that the goal is to make the old model leaner, not to build a new one.

In an MLG company, AI is not layered on top of the system. It is integrated into the reflexes that make the system viable. It allows pods to detect demand shifts before leadership sees them. It enables pricing adjustments without manual oversight. It powers execution loops that run on signal, not planning cycles. It compresses time between insight and action across every layer of GTM and product.

To understand how AI makes this possible, we need to move beyond surface-level use cases and examine its role across the five core functions of MLG execution: *sensing*, *interpreting*, *adapting*, *testing*, and *scaling*. In each, AI shifts the system from lagging to reflexive – from slow, top-down decision-making to decentralized, data-driven responsiveness.

## Section 1: Sensing – high-fidelity signal at scale

In traditional organizations, sensing the market is slow, filtered, and lagging. Data flows upward through layers of reporting, often aggregated and sanitized by the time leadership sees it. Strategic shifts are recognized after they have already manifested visibly – after customer behavior has changed, after competitors have captured new ground. In an MLG world, this delay is fatal.

Adaptive execution demands high-fidelity signals in real time. It requires companies not just to collect more data, but to ingest, interpret, and act on it faster than competitors. This is where AI-native sensing changes the operating model fundamentally. AI systems can process unstructured and structured data at scale, continuously surfacing weak signals before they consolidate into visible trends.

Rather than relying on quarterly business intelligence (BI) reports or lagging customer relationship management (CRM) snapshots, AI-driven MLG companies build shared intelligence layers that allow pods to detect changes directly, without waiting for interpretation from leadership.

## The anatomy of AI-native sensing

Leading MLG companies integrate multiple AI-driven tools into a live shared intelligence system. Other tools are available, and will depend on your use-case. The below are named only to give a sense of the capability-set you might want to consider.

- **Sales call intelligence**: Tools like *Gong.io* and *Chorus.ai* transcribe and analyze thousands of sales calls in real time, identifying emerging objections, feature requests, and competitive signals long before they appear in closed-lost reasons.
- **Social and sentiment monitoring**: Platforms like *Sprinklr*, *Brandwatch*, *Clay* continuously track conversations among target personas (e.g., CFOs) across LinkedIn, X (Twitter), and industry-specific forums – surfacing pain points, shifts in buyer priorities, and early competitive messaging changes.
- **Account engagement and intent data**: Systems like *6sense* and *Demandbase* detect when accounts are moving in-market, identifying shifts in intent signals before deal cycles even begin. AI-native CRMs like *Dreamhub.AI* collate elicit far greater understanding of prospect desires and customer needs.
- **Automated signal synthesis**: Tools like *Perplexity AI* and *ChatGPT Enterprise* synthesize diverse signal streams, automatically generating GTM insights – suggesting new positioning angles, identifying pricing risks, or surfacing feature gaps that pods can act on immediately.

In this model, pods are no longer dependent on centralized data teams producing retrospective analysis. Each pod operates as a live market sensor, adjusting execution based on continuous, real-world feedback.

## Why AI changes the economics of sensing

Historically, building high-fidelity sensing layers was prohibitively expensive. Human analysts could process only a fraction of the available data, and the cost of real-time monitoring at scale was unjustifiable for most mid-sized companies. AI obliterates this constraint. Systems now operate continuously, processing millions of signals at marginal cost, identifying not only what is happening, but *what is beginning to happen* – the early pattern shifts that are invisible to traditional reporting structures.

This compresses the sensing cycle from quarters to days, sometimes hours. Mid-market CFO pods, for instance, might detect a spike in demand for AI-powered cash flow forecasting within a week of initial conversations, adjusting positioning long before slower-moving competitors realize the shift. Sensing becomes a living reflex, not a quarterly report.

## Section 2: Deciding – autonomous, context-aware recommendations

MLG organizations do not just sense faster; they decide faster. AI-native execution enables context-aware decision-making loops that operate at the edge of the organization – where pods detect shifts and act reflexively, within strategic boundaries, without waiting for centralized validation. The goal is not to eliminate leadership oversight. It is to ensure that leadership governs the system's parameters while AI accelerates operational decisions inside those parameters.

### The structure of AI-native decision making

An effective AI-native decision system does three things: it interprets context, recommends actions within boundaries, and escalates edge cases.

### Contextual interpretation

AI doesn't just surface data – it interprets it in context. Systems like *Clari* and *People.ai* track pipeline velocity and deal health, flagging not just what's off-track but why – delayed multithreading, procurement friction, or a pricing mismatch. Instead of raw dashboards, pods receive decision-ready insights.

### Guardrailed recommendations

AI generates next-best actions – adjusting pricing, shifting GTM strategy, reallocating accounts – bounded by constraints like margin, capacity, or regulatory policy. Vendors like *Zilliant* and *Pigment* offer scenario modelling and real-time pricing guidance, while platforms like *Drift's* AI sales assistants tailor prospect engagement based on intent and account tier.

### Automated escalation

Not every call can – or should – be made autonomously. When a decision strays outside safe parameters (say, a discount that breaches profit floor or messaging that risks compliance exposure), AI systems (likely internally built into and around existing systems) escalate to humans for review. This blend keeps pods agile but aligned with broader strategy.

In this model, pods no longer wait for leadership to interpret signals or approve every course correction. They operate inside a pre-designed 'decision space,' where AI ensures decisions remain aligned to strategy while removing the latency of manual review cycles.

### Why AI-native deciding matters for reflex speed

The speed of the decision cycle directly determines the reflex quality of an MLG organization. No matter how fast sensing becomes, if every adjustment requires cross-functional alignment meetings or escalations through traditional approval hierarchies, adaptability collapses under the weight of decision-making processes.

AI-native decision systems compress the time between market signal and action-ready decision. They also adjust the location of decisions. They allow pods to adjust before competitors detect the need to adjust. They preserve strategic coherence without reintroducing top-down bottlenecks that undermine decentralized execution.

Leadership's role shifts from making individual decisions to designing and maintaining the system that makes fast, bounded decisions continuously.

## Section 3: Executing – dynamic, data-driven action loops

Sensing and deciding create potential. Execution converts potential into market advantage. In traditional organizations, even when decisions are made correctly, the act of execution often introduces fatal delays. Campaigns must pass through creative reviews. Pricing changes require weeks of systems updates. Sales enablement is updated quarterly. In an MLG organization, execution must operate at the same speed as sensing and deciding – or the reflex system collapses.

AI-native execution replaces manual activation delays with dynamic, data-driven action loops. Once a decision is made – whether by a human, by AI, or collaboratively – execution happens reflexively, governed by shared systems that automate adjustment across GTM functions in real time.

### The mechanics of AI-native execution

In an MLG organization, execution is not queued behind cross-functional processes. It is triggered by live systems designed to translate decisions into action instantly:

- **Dynamic pricing adjustments**: Systems like *Reveni*, *Pricefx*, and *Flintfox* enable pricing updates to propagate automatically across billing systems, sales enablement platforms, and customer-facing quotes – without requiring manual reconciliation or new contract cycles.
- **Sales enablement updates**: Platforms like *Mindset.AI* can push updated playbooks, pricing guidance, and messaging variations directly into front-line sales workflows, ensuring that sellers are not just acting on the latest intelligence without lag, but can engage with it interactively rather than as 'new updated slides'.
- **Marketing campaign adaptation**: The major marketing platforms (Marketo, etc.) when layered with AI recommendation and delivery engines like *Blueshift*, *SeventhSense* or *Onespot* dynamically adjust content, messaging, and segmentation based on live customer engagement signals.
- **Product feature deployment**: Tools like *LaunchDarkly* and *Split.io* allow product teams to deploy feature flags or modify in-app experiences based on AI-prioritized feedback loops – without requiring full product releases or engineering sprints.

In this system, the 'hand-off' from sensing and deciding to execution is not a manual relay race. It is a dynamic trigger network, where actions ripple outward immediately once a validated signal or decision crosses the threshold.

### Why execution reflex defines competitive tempo

In adaptive markets, the quality of execution is increasingly measured not by plan compliance, but by latency – the time between recognizing a need and acting on it in the market. Companies that still require multiple approval layers, manual campaign retooling, or engineering escalations to adjust basic go-to-market (GTM) tactics will always lag behind AI-native operators.

Execution reflex is where MLG organizations win. Not by planning better, but by acting faster – at the same quality level. Pods operating within an AI-native execution loop can respond to customer needs, competitive moves, or market shifts within days, sometimes hours. Competitors executing on traditional quarterly cycles cannot.

# Section 4: Learning – closing the loop without lag

In a traditional company, learning is episodic and slow. Insights from customer feedback, competitive shifts, or execution failures accumulate quietly, only to be reviewed quarterly, or worse, annually. By the time learning translates into a plan adjustment, the original market conditions that triggered the learning have already changed. In an MLG company, that cycle is inverted. Learning is continuous, operational, and built into the reflex of the system itself.

AI-native execution transforms learning from a retrospective exercise into a live operational feedback loop. Every action taken – every pricing adjustment, every sales engagement, every marketing experiment – feeds new data back into the system. That data is not stored for future review; it is ingested, analyzed, and operationalized in near real time.

## How AI-native learning loops operate

In a fully integrated MLG system, AI continuously monitors the results of execution, extracting insights without waiting for manual analysis:

- **Campaign optimization**: Systems like *Mutiny* and *Iterable* dynamically adjust website personalization, content offers, and outbound messaging based on live engagement signals – not after a full campaign cycle, but during active execution.
- **Product usage feedback**: Platforms like *Heap* and *Amplitude* surface behavioral insights on feature adoption, retention patterns, and user friction immediately, allowing product

teams to reprioritize development efforts without requiring executive backlog reviews.

- **Pricing and revenue impact**: Tools like *Pricefx* and *ChurnZero* provide live analytics on how pricing adjustments and customer success interventions are impacting revenue, churn, and margin – feeding actionable data directly back to GTM and finance teams.

Instead of leadership waiting for post-mortem decks, or pods waiting for quarterly strategy summits, learning flows back into the system continuously, updating execution automatically where the signal is strong enough – or flagging to humans where judgment is still required.

### *Why closing the learning loop changes execution quality*

The quality of an adaptive organization is defined not just by how fast it moves, but by how fast it improves. In an MLG system, every iteration – every customer interaction, product feature release, pricing test – becomes a live experiment with embedded instrumentation. Companies still operating on quarterly retrospectives are building strategies on expired information. MLG companies are building strategies on today's verified results.

## Section 5: Scaling – autonomous pods and AI-to-AI coordination

Everything we've described in this chapter so far – AI-enabled sensing, decision-making, execution, and learning – makes MLG operationally viable. But scale introduces new complexity. As companies expand across markets, segments, and geographies, execution speed is often lost to coordination cost – messaging fragments. pricing inconsistencies emerge, product development becomes reactive – the reflexes that once gave the business its edge begin to dull under the weight of growth.

In an MLG company, scaling is not about standardizing execution, it's about distributing reflex. AI makes this possible by absorbing coordination cost across decentralized pods, enabling each to move fast while remaining strategically aligned. The real opportunity – still nascent, but increasingly within reach – is intelligent, autonomous systems coordinating directly with one another, adjusting execution without waiting for human mediation.

## The promise and acceleration of agentic AI

The idea of agentic AI – autonomous systems acting on behalf of humans and interacting with other autonomous systems – is no longer speculative. In early 2025, OpenAI launched memory-enabled, agent-capable versions of ChatGPT, turning what had been a conversational interface into something far closer to a semi-autonomous digital employee. These GPTs can retain context over time, call tools, chain actions, and participate in workflows across days or weeks.

Around them, a fast-growing ecosystem is emerging: large language models (LLM) plugins now integrate with enterprise software, triggering actions across CRMs, ERPs, and ticketing systems. Early-stage platforms like Mindset.AI, Cognosys, Lindy, and Rewind are layering orchestration on top, building agents that not only generate content or answer questions, but initiate and complete business processes end-to-end. This is the frontier: AI no longer as interface or assistant, but as collaborator – sometimes as manager of other AIs.

In that context, the scenarios we've previously framed are no longer hypothetical:

- AI-powered customer support doesn't just answer tickets – it resolves them by interfacing with logistics platforms, issuing refunds, or triggering replacements autonomously.
- Procurement AIs don't just shortlist vendors – they actively negotiate with vendor-side AIs on delivery windows and volume discounts.
- Pricing AIs don't just recommend adjustments – they deploy them in real time across SKUs, based on competitor moves inferred from scraping public data.

Of course, this is still early-stage tech. Reliability remains variable. Governance, transparency, and explainability are live concerns – especially in regulated sectors. Most companies are not, and should not be, handing over high-stakes decisions to autonomous agents just yet.

But the direction of travel is unmistakable – and accelerating. Agentic infrastructure will redefine not just how individual tasks get done, but how coordination happens at scale. The organizations that begin to restructure their systems, roles, and workflows with AI-to-AI execution in mind won't just be ready when the tech matures. They'll mature with it.

## Why AI enables scalable reflex

In legacy models, scaling execution requires scaling people: more marketing managers, more sales enablement, more analysts, more approvals. In an AI-native MLG model, scaling execution does not require scaling headcount linearly. Instead, shared AI infrastructure allows pods to self-adjust – autonomously updating messaging, pricing, prioritization, and product feedback without introducing bottlenecks or duplication.

As this infrastructure matures, even more of the coordination effort will be absorbed by machines:

- Product feedback from one pod becomes instantly available and actionable in another.
- Successful pricing experiments in one geography trigger test iterations in adjacent markets.
- Emerging competitor positioning is countered by automated GTM shifts coordinated across pods.

Over time, the reflexes that once relied on structured playbooks and executive review cycles are embedded into shared systems – making the company not just faster, but *self-correcting* at scale.

### The strategic horizon: Governance before capability

The companies that win in this next phase won't be the ones with simply the most advanced models. They'll be the ones that understand where AI-autonomy is safe, where human-escalation is necessary, and how to build systems that earn trust before they demand it as a fact of their existence.

- Where can AI safely execute without oversight?
- When must decisions escalate to humans?
- What guardrails are in place to prevent small misalignments from compounding into systemic risk?

Answering these questions well will matter more than algorithmic performance. In the early stages of agentic AI, *governance is strategy*.

## Conclusion: AI-native execution completes the system

MLG demands more than new ideas about teams, metrics, or cadence. It demands execution systems capable of adapting as fast as the market shifts – and capable of scaling without slowing down. AI is what makes that system viable. Not because it replaces human expertise, but because it amplifies it – reducing the latency between signal and action, enabling faster cycles of learning, and allowing pods to operate as true reflexive units.

But AI doesn't make growth easier, it makes speed possible, and speed, without structure, becomes chaos. What matters now is not just how fast individual pods can react – but how many pods a company can coordinate without collapsing under its own weight.

That is the final challenge MLG must solve: *how to scale the model*. Not with bloat, complexity, or centralization – but with precision, agility, and alignment. The answer is not just organizational – it's architectural. The next two chapters outline how this can be done. First, in Chapter 11, how to build your very first market pod, and then, Chapter 12 introduces how to go further with *fractal scaling*. It is the pattern that makes MLG scalable – without losing what makes it work.

# Part III

# Implementing
# Market-Led Growth

# 11

# Building your first perpetual product-market fit loop

## Introduction: Start with one loop, not a transformation

By now, the idea should be clear: Market-Led Growth (MLG) is an operating model for companies navigating volatility and AI disruption. But you don't have to overhaul everything at once. MLG starts small – with execution. This chapter is about how to begin that execution – where to start, what to build, and how to do it without triggering immune responses that kill the work before it proves its value.

You don't implement MLG across an entire company. Unless you're starting from scratch, that lift would be too hard. Instead, you construct a single perpetual product-market fit (PMF) loop – fully operational, independently resourced, and fast enough to respond to real-time market shifts – then you run that loop, then you scale.

### The loop you are building

As a reminder, refer to Figure 20 to see what the loop looks like.

This is not a quarterly review cycle. It is a living, breathing feedback loop designed to keep you aligned to a moving target: market fit. Done right, it replaces the traditional planning-to-execution pipeline with a real-time cycle of signal, response, and iteration.

**Sense**

Detect changes in buyer
behavior, usage patterns,
sentiment, or signal.

**Scale**

If it works, double
down. If it fails, log the
learning and kill it.

**Perpetual
product-
market-fit
(PMF) cycle**

**Interpret**

Understand what those shifts
imply for your positioning,
pricing, product, or motion.

**Test**

Run the smallest
version of the idea that
proves or disproves it.

**Adapt**

Make changes. Quickly.
Offer structure, copy, GTM
motion, pricing.

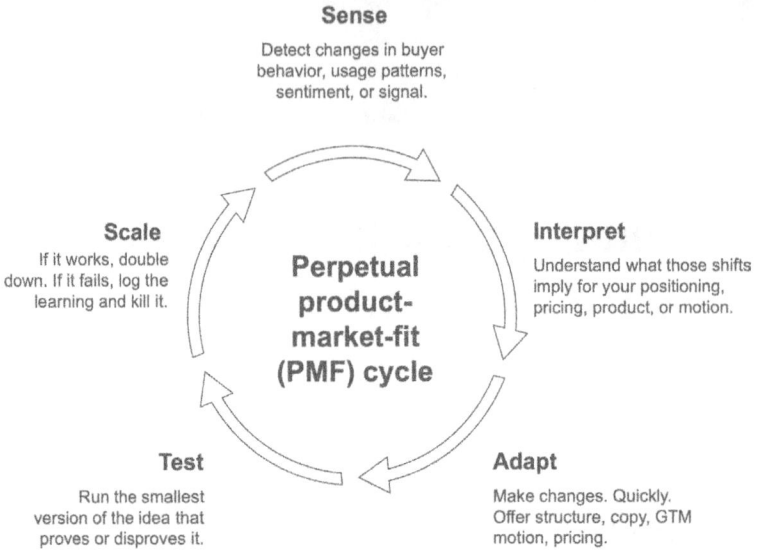

**Figure 20** This loop looks big and scary but it really doesn't have to be. Start small, learn, iterate, and scale when you're ready. Stay the course, it's worth it.

The rest of this chapter walks through how to build a team that runs this loop end to end. Not as a pilot, not as a prototype, and not as an isolated growth team. As a fully empowered go-to-market (GTM) unit. This is where MLG starts – not in a strategy deck, but in the action of a pod that senses, decides, executes, and learns on its own clock speed.

## This will challenge you

If you're in a leadership position, the process will feel unfamiliar. That's not incidental, it's a requirement. The defining feature of traditional GTM execution – whether sales-led, product-led, or marketing-led – is centralized decision-making. MLG removes that definition. You are instead building a system where the people closest to the signal are empowered to act on it immediately. Which means things will happen without your approval – messaging will change, experiments will run, pricing will shift – and none of it will wait for consensus.

That is not a loss of control, it is the reallocation of decision rights in service of speed, and speed, in this market, is what separates those who adapt from those who decline.

The first time you do this, it will feel like too much and that's normal. The companies that succeed in this transition are not the ones that get every detail right from the start. They're the ones that commit fully to the premise: that adaptability is the only sustainable advantage, and that the fastest way to prove it is to build the system and run it.

So, one loop, one team, one market segment (or one geography, or one customer-type). Let's start there.

## Step 1: Build the pod that runs the loop

### Execution begins with the right container

The perpetual PMF loop runs on people – specifically, on a team that has the mandate and the means to move. Before you embed real-time sensing, before you launch experiments, before you adapt a single message, you need to construct the unit that will carry the work. That unit is the pod, scoped tightly around a single market segment or motion, and given full autonomy to run the PMF loop end to end: sense → interpret → adapt → test → scale. It is not there to make recommendations. It is there to take action.

The success or failure of MLG begins here. If you design the pod well, the system works. If you get this step wrong – if the pod is too big, too slow, or too entangled in legacy dependencies – MLG will stall before it ever starts.

### Start where things are breaking, not somewhere new

The most effective place to launch your first pod is not where things are going well, it's where they're beginning to break. Not in crisis, but in pattern.

Look for GTM motions that were working and now aren't – where customer acquisition costs (CAC) are creeping up, conversion rates are drifting down, sales cycles are stretching, or competitive losses are rising. Look for buyer behavior that feels suddenly unfamiliar. Where your team is still running the same playbook, but the market has stopped responding to it. This is not a failure. It's a signal that product-market fit is moving – and that your current system is not keeping up.

These friction points are where MLG can be implemented first. The goal is not to patch the old motion, it's to replace it with one that adapts in real time. The pod exists to build a live, responsive system on top of that friction, using it as fuel.

Avoid launching your first pod in a brand-new market – the risk is too high. If the team is learning the market, the buyer, and the operating model all at once, you won't know what's actually driving the results. Choose a known segment with enough traction to generate signal, but enough instability to justify change.

## Scope tightly: Design for independence

The pod should be scoped tightly enough to reduce noise, but large enough to own outcomes. Think in terms of discrete motions: a specific vertical, an identifiable buyer type, a high-potential use case. One pod might focus on mid-market CFOs in Europe, the Middle East, and Africa (EMEA). Another on converting usage from free to paid in a single product line. The tighter the scope, the faster the learning loop.

But scope alone is not enough, the pod must also be structurally independent. That means it does not rely on approvals from functions outside the team. If a messaging test needs brand signoff, or a pricing experiment needs to route through legal, the loop breaks. You are not building a matrix team, you are building a fast-adapting cell. Execution authority must sit inside the pod. Realized speed is rarely a function of urgency, it is a function of design.

## Staff for reflexes, not representation

The pod does not need to be a miniature version of your entire GTM org. It needs just the core capabilities of the MLG cycle:

- **Sensing**: Someone who uses the systems in the last chapter to track signal flow from customers, competitors, usage, and behavior.
- **Adapting and interpretation**: Someone who can translate that signal into testable hypotheses and prioritized changes.
- **Test (and scale)**: One or more people who can act: launch campaigns, rewrite messaging, adjust pricing, run outbound, or deploy product-level changes.
- **Instrumentation**: Someone (or a shared AI system) who can track outcomes and feed learnings back into the loop.

Each of these roles must come with execution rights. If they don't have the authority to act, they're just observers. That is the difference between a reporting function and a learning system. This is not about perfect structure, it is about functional completeness. You are building a system that can sense and respond without waiting for instructions.

## What this team is for

This pod is the future, built at a small scale. Its job is not to make recommendations to the executive team. Its job is to ship execution that proves or disproves live hypotheses. Its success will not be measured in whether the leadership team liked it, or other functions got along with it, but in speed of learning and market responsiveness. You are not looking for linear progress, you are looking for reflexes.

If the pod runs the loop successfully, it earns the right to replicate. If it doesn't, it will show you exactly where the bottlenecks are in your current system. Either way, it's valuable. This is where MLG starts: not with a new vision, but with a functioning loop. Start small, start fast, and start where the friction already is.

# Step 2: Sense – install a (small) shared intelligence stack

## All the data, even the messy stuff

This is where most companies fail: they only feed the sensing system the data that's already been sanitized – deal outcomes, aggregated survey results, website metrics from approved dashboards – but you cannot detect shifts in the market using only the data your teams have already labeled as important. You don't know what the pattern is until it emerges – and by then, it's too late to go back and collect the raw inputs that would've revealed it earlier.

If you're serious about MLG, everything goes in. Raw Gong transcripts, not just call summaries. Unstructured customer relationship management (CRM) notes, including the typos. Free-text objections logged by reps who weren't thinking about analytics. Product telemetry that hasn't been rolled up into KPIs yet. That data feels noisy, it is, that's why it matters. The pattern lives in the noise – until it doesn't.

Here's the practical implication: you need a sensing system that's built to handle full-fidelity input. Which means you need to rethink how you're using AI.

## Use a localized LLM as your signal engine

Off-the-shelf AI tools are useful for summarization. But if you want a durable sensing layer inside your pod – one that can safely ingest sensitive inputs like sales performance data, usage anomalies, churn flags, and competitive mentions – you'll need to run a localized large language model (LLM).

That doesn't mean building from scratch. There are open-source models (Llama 3, Mistral, Mixtral) that can be fine-tuned on internal data and deployed in your own environment. A mid-size software-as-a-service (SaaS) company I worked with, for instance, fine-tuned a Mistral 7B model on six months of Gong calls, CRM notes, and support chat logs. Within a week, the model began clustering recurring drop-off objections that hadn't been tagged by reps and weren't flagged in win/loss reports. The insight: a single configuration issue in onboarding was quietly killing deal momentum. That's the point of the system – to find the issue before it becomes 'official.'

Use a localized model because you control the data. You can load it with the messy, risky, politically sensitive stuff your teams don't want to put into a slide, and you can train it to look for weak signals, not just summarize what already happened.

Weekly, the pod should feed new data in: fresh transcripts, flagged Slack threads, new usage segments. This isn't overhead – it's upkeep. If your sensing model is stale, your loop will be blind.

## Build the practice, not just the stack

Technology won't solve the problem if the team isn't using it. The pod must build sensing into its rhythm. Every week, the pod should be looking at what changed: in language, in objections, in segment behavior, in conversion curves. Don't bury this inside a 'review' meeting – make it a working session – what's moving, and what does it suggest?

Structure it lightly:

- Each pod member brings one piece of signal worth noting.
- The LLM flags trend deltas or unusual co-occurrences.
- You identify one hypothesis worth exploring in the next sprint.

## Everyone is a sensor

In a traditional GTM model, 'insight' is centralized – usually in product marketing, product ops, or a strategy function. In an MLG pod, sensing is collective. Everyone contributes. Everyone has eyes on the market.

Sales development representatives (SDRs) hear the new objections first. Customer success managers (CSMs) notice when usage patterns shift. Engineers spot API workarounds. The system is only as smart as the edge inputs it receives.

That means two things:

1. **Create a single input layer**: A shared Slack channel, a Notion log, a centralized insight repo – something every pod member can contribute to and draw from.
2. **Don't gate contributions**: If a junior rep flags something that seems small, don't dismiss it. Repetition validates pattern, but detection starts with someone noticing a single deviation.

Over time, this builds a culture where signal is expected and reflected upon – not escalated.

## Better awareness is a competitive advantage

Most companies optimize execution. Fewer optimize perception. But awareness is what makes speed valuable. Without signal, you're just running faster into irrelevance.

The companies that win in volatile markets are not just the ones that act quickly. They're the ones that see clearly, early. Your pod's ability to detect market drift before it hits your metrics is the difference between adapting in time – or apologizing in hindsight.

So, treat sensing as core infrastructure, make it real-time, feed it everything, train the team to contribute, and trust the system when it starts to see around corners. You've built the pod and you've wired in the radar, now it's time to interpret what it's telling you.

# Step 3: Interpret – translate signal into hypothesis

## Decide fast: You'll learn more by shipping than by speculating

Signal alone doesn't create advantage. Most just don't know what to do with it. The role of interpretation is to bridge the gap between perception and action. It's where the pod turns insight into execution – not by building consensus or waiting for perfect clarity, but by forming hypotheses fast and getting them to market even faster.

If your team waits until it's sure, it will never move fast enough. In an MLG system, interpretation doesn't mean building a case. It means deciding what to try next.

## Go from hypothesis to test, fast: That's the move

At this point, you've built the pod and wired in the radar. New signals are coming in: pricing objections, usage anomalies, buyer hesitations. The mistake most teams make here is to pause, they overthink, they chase internal validation, they try to turn signal into strategy – when the loop just needs a test.

Interpretation means framing the signal into a hypothesis and attaching a real-world action to it. That's it.

- **Hypothesis**: What do we think is shifting?
- **Trial**: What will we do to find out if we're right?

This doesn't require certainty, it requires clarity – a message to test, a price to vary, a call script to tweak, an outbound hook to rewrite. You don't prove it in the room – you prove it in the field.

Say your pod is seeing an uptick in sales objections around implementation complexity. Your hypothesis might be: 'Buyers are hesitating because they don't believe we'll deliver value in the first 30 days.' The corresponding test could be as simple as: 'Run a revised outbound campaign emphasizing time-to-value in the first month. Track engagement and conversion delta over five days.'

That's the loop. Not a six-week initiative. Not a positioning workshop. A live test, running by next Monday.

## You don't need one great hypothesis: You need ten working ones

The goal here is not brilliance, it's motion. Most teams try to get the hypothesis right before acting. MLG pods act to find out what's right.

You don't need to predict the winner – you need to keep the loop turning. That means volume matters. The pod should be generating multiple hypotheses per cycle. Not all of them will lead to breakthroughs, and they're not supposed to, but every hypothesis that gets tested increases your failure yield ratio (FYR) – the percentage of failed bets that still generate useful learning.

That's one of the metrics that matters in an MLG system. Not how often you win, but how often you learn something you can use next time. Another is market activation speed (MAS) – the time it takes from noticing a shift to having a response live in market. That speed doesn't come from pre-baked answers, it comes from a team that's trained to turn ambiguity into action without getting stuck in analysis.

You don't need to be right often (although that would be a bonus). You need to be wrong usefully – and fast enough to act again.

## Use AI to accelerate the framing – not to replace It

AI is useful here. It can cluster signals, summarize sentiment, suggest language, and even propose next-step variations. But don't confuse that with decision-making. What AI is good at is reducing friction: speeding up the path from raw input to structured hypothesis. What it's bad at is judgment.

You still need the team to decide: Does this signal matter? Is this hypothesis credible? Is this response worth testing? The best pods will AI to do >80% of the grunt work – then make the final call with human judgment sharpened by proximity to the customer.

This is where you separate signal from noise. Not by adding rigor, but by shipping something that will tell you what's actually true.

### Build the reflex: 'What are we going to try?'

Interpretation should be a standing rhythm inside the pod. When new signal lands – whether from AI, a field report, or a shift in conversion curves – the next question is automatic: What are we going to try? Crucially, not: how do we escalate this? Not: How do we validate this? Not: How do we get approval to act on this?

Just: *What's the smallest, fastest experiment that would show us if this is real?* Make hypothesis-logging visible. Set a rhythm. For example, you might decide that each week, the pod should have at least one new live test in play and another one queued. Track the cadence. Share what was learned. Don't measure success by accuracy – measure it by learning velocity.

If the pod gets good at this – if it develops the muscle to turn weak signals into real-world hypotheses without waiting for someone to make the case – then the rest of the loop becomes inevitable. So don't stop at the insight. Move. You'll find out what's true when the numbers come back.

## Step 4: Adapt and test – run small, fast changes in market

This is where the model gets tested – and where most teams flinch.

Once the pod has formed a hypothesis, the next move is adaptation. This is where the loop crosses the line from sensing and thinking to doing. Something changes in market. A real shift in message, offer, channel, or positioning – visible to customers, not just internally discussed.

Done well, this is where the pod starts to come into its own. If you've built it right – tight scope, clear decision rights, proximity to signal – then it can now move faster than the rest of the organization. This is the moment it was designed for, but this is also where MLG is at its most fragile, because early adaptations rarely work the first time, and that's exactly the point.

## Early failure is not a sign of a broken model

When the first few adaptations fall flat, stakeholders will notice. You changed the pricing structure – and conversion didn't move. You updated the call script – and objections stayed flat. You launched a new messaging test – and engagement dropped. These are not anomalies, they are the cost of movement, but to observers who are still operating from a playbook mindset, they look like failure. They look like proof that MLG is risky: indecisive and inefficient.

If you are leading this pod – or leading the introduction of MLG into the business – this is where you earn your credibility. You must hold the line because this is the moment the system is most likely to be abandoned.

The temptation will be to pull back, to wait for more evidence, and to get 'alignment' before trying again.

### *Don't give in to temptation*

This is exactly when you double down. You remind the team – and your stakeholders – that MLG is not a prediction engine. It's a learning system. The value of adaptation isn't that it always works. It's that it produces new signal when it doesn't.

This is why we measure the FYR – because the job is not to avoid being wrong – it's to learn as much as possible, as fast as possible, from what doesn't work, and it's why we measure MAS – because the ability to respond quickly is itself the competitive advantage. The company that runs four unsuccessful tests this quarter learns more than the company that waits for one big move. So, when adaptations fail, don't back off, instead, show that the system is doing its job.

## Run it live, keep it light

Adaptation doesn't require a full relaunch. It can do – but not every swing needs to be a big one. There is lots of value in small fast, deliberate swings – repeatedly.

Examples:

- Rewrite the headline and subhead on your pricing page to reflect a new ROI framing.
- Insert a new objection-handling line into outbound email step 2 and track response.
- Reorder the benefits on a pitch deck slide to reflect updated buyer priorities.
- Launch a new offer variant to one ideal customer profile (ICP) segment only, via paid social.
- Test a different CTA language on your enterprise landing page.

These are not 'initiatives,' they are adaptations, and they must be real. If it doesn't touch the customer, it doesn't count. The scope should be tight. But the deployment must be live.

This is where a lot of companies fake the loop. They draft messaging internally. They model price changes. They rework slide decks in Figma but don't send them into the field. That's not adaptation, that's rehearsal, and it teaches you nothing. Adaptation is not analysis, it's execution with intent.

## Action is the only way to know

Once a hypothesis is formed, and the cost of testing is low, the pod should act. Not next month. Not after a review. Now. This is the difference between a pod that's just observing the market and a pod that's actively moving with it.

Use the autonomy you've already built into the pod. That was the point. The pod doesn't need permission to act on signal. If it does, you haven't built a pod – you've built another function with extra meetings.

This is where the system starts to stretch, where decision rights are real, where leadership has to trust the loop more than they trust their own instinct, and where the rest of the company starts to watch closely. Which brings us to your role.

### If you're leading this, this is where you lead

If you are the executive sponsor of MLG – formally or informally – this is where you need to be present. You need to be seen defending the model before it delivers perfect outcomes. You need to be the one reminding the team that early tests are supposed to be inconclusive. You need to redirect internal conversations away from 'did it work?' and toward 'what did we learn?' and 'how fast can we move?'

Because this is the moment where the company will be most tempted to regress – to the safety of planning cycles, the familiarity of consensus, the illusion of control. You have to hold your nerve. This part will not look clean. But you are building muscle.

You are teaching the system to move, and no system learns to move without first learning to fall. If you can get the organization through this phase – if you can normalize rapid, imperfect adaptation – then the next phase becomes not just possible, but inevitable. Because now you're learning what works.

And it's time to scale.

## Step 5: Scale – double down on what works, kill what doesn't

This is not the reward, it's the responsibility. Scaling is where most companies start. In MLG, it's where you arrive.

By the time a pod reaches this point, it has sensed a shift, framed a hypothesis, adapted a tactic, and deployed it in market. Now, it has real results – behavioral, commercial, measurable. Some things will have worked, but most won't. The work now is to decide what to do with that data – and to act decisively. Not just in accelerating what's effective, but in shutting down what isn't. Because nothing kills learning faster than letting failure linger.

This is the end of the loop, and it's what gives the loop power. You scale what the market validates, and you kill what it doesn't. Then you go again.

## Don't wait to kill: Do it first

Start here: kill the underperforming tests, not with humiliation, but with precision. Every adaptation you launched – every message variant, price test, offer format – should have had a clear kill condition baked in: 'If this hasn't moved [x] within [y] timeframe, we stop it.' If you didn't define one, define it now. Because until you end the failed test, your system is still wasting energy on it. The learning is done. Move on.

This matters not just operationally, but culturally. Killing weak plays quickly shows that speed is valued over sunk cost. That action is better than defensiveness. That failure is not just tolerated – it's expected and managed.

When pods start hiding slow performers or 'giving them another sprint,' that's not experimentation, that's politics, and it's the fastest way to collapse the trust that made the loop possible in the first place. So, kill fast, learn, document the failed hypothesis and what it taught you. Move the team's attention to the next iteration. In MLG, failure isn't the tax – it's the raw material.

## Scaling is not a celebration: It's a system

When something works, don't celebrate it. Scale it.

In most organizations, success creates pause: people want to debrief, write a case study, present it to leadership. That instinct is understandable – and wrong. Every hour spent packaging success is an hour you could be using to multiply it.

Scaling means reallocation, not recognition. Move budget. Move people. Push the winning tactic into new segments. Lift the language that worked in one campaign and use AI to adapt it for three others. Expand the test, then expand again.

The window of competitive advantage is short. You are not the only company sensing the shift. If the market has validated something – through response, conversion, retention – your job is not to admire it. Your job is to distribute it before anyone else does.

This is why MAS doesn't stop at test launch. It also applies to test propagation. If it takes two weeks to approve budget to scale a validated play, you're giving the market a head start on your own insight.

## AI is the scaling engine

This is where AI delivers asymmetric leverage. When a test works, AI should be wired to:

- Clone messaging variants for similar ICPs.
- Push updates to related pods or field teams.
- Generate supporting collateral automatically.
- Suggest adjacent segments showing similar behavior patterns.

Scaling doesn't have to be big, but it has to be immediate. You don't need a marketing team to rebuild the deck. You need AI to generate the slide, rewrite the email, and launch the sequence – today. The loop that can scale autonomously is the loop that compounds.

## What you don't scale matters just as much

Not everything should move forward. Even successful experiments can be local artifacts – something that worked because of a quirk in timing, audience, or context. You don't need to push everything up. You need to know what not to push.

That's why pods must review not just the results, but the replicability. Did it work because it solved a root problem, or because it landed on a temporary pain point? Did it unlock strategic insight, or tactical lift? You scale plays that reflect durable shifts in demand – not lucky breaks.

## Build the system to share, not just to succeed

As you scale, the goal is not just to grow one pod's success, it's to create shared leverage across the MLG network. The real outcome here isn't more pipeline, it's institutional learning.

That requires structure:

- A shared pattern library of what worked and why.
- Lightweight processes for distributing validated plays.
- Automatic circulation of top performers across pods, geos, or functions.
- Regular synthesis of what's working – driven by data, not ego.

Scaling in MLG is not a victory lap, it's the reload cycle. You scale so you can move the next pod faster. You scale so the company doesn't waste time reinventing what's already been proven, and then you return to the loop. Because, by now, the market has already started to move again.

# From one loop to many – scaling MLG beyond the first pod

## Loops don't grow by getting bigger: They multiply

If you've built your first pod well – tight scope, strong reflexes, disciplined rhythm – it will show you what's possible. That alone is valuable. Most companies never get a real view of what adaptation at speed looks like in practice. But one loop, however effective, is not the model, it's the prototype.

The power of MLG is not in what a single team can do. It's in what happens when multiple teams, running in parallel, begin sensing, adapting, and learning faster than the rest of the market. That's the next phase, and it doesn't begin by hiring more people. It begins by replicating the conditions that made the first pod work.

## Don't scale the org: Scale the conditions

It's easy to misunderstand what you're trying to scale. You're not building a new department or layering in another GTM process. You're building a distributed system – one where each loop runs independently, but with shared infrastructure and common principles.

What made the first pod effective wasn't headcount. It was environment:

- Local autonomy to act on signal.
- Real-time access to market data.
- A culture of experimentation, not perfection.
- Clear kill/scale rules.
- Leadership that backed velocity over consensus.

When you build the second pod, and the third, your job isn't to duplicate structure. It's to recreate those conditions, and to protect them as the system grows.

## The people you add matter more than the structure you scale

By now, you know what kind of people thrive in this model. You've seen it up close: the team members who didn't wait for permission – who challenged the signal, but still acted. Who moved fast, failed visibly, and stayed focused on what was next. These people aren't common. But they are critical. They don't just operate in the loop – they embody it.

As you scale, you need more of them. That means hiring for orientation, not just experience:

- Do they move without a roadmap?
- Do they learn faster than they defend?
- Can they interpret ambiguity without freezing?

These are not resume traits, they're execution traits, and they determine whether the next pods move faster – or simply repeat the old habits with new titles. What you're scaling is not a methodology, it's a mindset. The pod is just the container.

## Who won't survive in an MLG pod?

Just as important as knowing who to hire is knowing who will kill your MLG initiative before it starts. The following mindsets are lethal:

- **The playbook follower**: Needs everything to be structured, follows a strict GTM process, struggles with ambiguity.
- **The approval seeker**: Hesitates to launch tests without sign-off, waits for meetings instead of executing.
- **The data hoarder**: Prefers to collect insights rather than act on them, wants 'more proof' before making a move.
- **The risk avoider**: Optimizes for safe, known ways of doing things, rather than high-speed adaptation.
- **The over-planner**: Wants to map out experiments in detail before starting, instead of iterating in real time.

If you see these behaviors in someone, they do not belong in your first MLG pod.

## Scale weakens structure: Unless you defend it

There's a moment in every transformation where growth threatens fidelity. As more pods form, the system gets noisier, and the results vary. Successes don't replicate cleanly. Someone suggests standardizing the messaging. Someone else proposes a central approval path for pricing tests. Leadership starts asking why every pod works differently.

This is the moment you planned for because MLG is not efficient, it's adaptive, and that means the system will always feel slightly out of sync – because it's responding to things the rest of the company hasn't noticed yet.

You don't fix this by making pods uniform. You fix it by reinforcing what made them fast: shared visibility, decentralized execution, and trust in the loop. Variability is not a flaw, it's the system telling you what's shifting – and where.

## Leadership's role shifts again

When the first pod launched, your job was to protect it. To explain the model. To defend its early failures and show what learning looked like in motion. As you scale, your job changes – you become a conductor – not of outputs, but of flow.

You make signal visible across pods, you fund the fast movers, you remove the bottlenecks that slow teams down – not by directing them, but by clearing the road ahead. You don't own the results, you own the rhythm. At this point, MLG is no longer a GTM experiment. It's the operating cadence of your company.

## From loops to systems

This chapter was about proving the loop. Running one pod, with one mandate, in a single segment – end to end. What comes next is what happens when that loop becomes the default rhythm of the organization. When every part of your GTM, and eventually your product and operations teams, begin running adaptive loops of their own.

The kind of alignment that emerges as you scale is fractal. That's what happens in the transition from model to system. So how does that work?

12

# Fractal growth: Scaling
# a Market-Led Growth business

## Introduction: Growth without bloat

For most companies, scaling means getting bigger – bigger teams, bigger budgets, bigger departments. Growth is measured in headcount, revenue expansion, and geographical footprint. But this kind of growth – the kind that prioritizes size over agility – has become a trap.

The more a company scales in this way, the more unwieldy it becomes. Leaders who once spent their time shaping market strategy and talking to customers now find themselves managing internal politics, navigating budget approvals, and handling personnel issues. What started as a sharp, focused go-to-market (GTM) motion gradually bloats as more team members are added, leading to an expanded ideal customer profile (ICP), diluted positioning, and an increasingly inefficient machine.

Instead of growth being the result of strong execution, it becomes the objective in itself. Teams expand not because there is a clear, validated path to optimal product-market fit (PMF), but because it's simply what scaling companies are expected to do. The result? Slower decision-making, less adaptability, and a loss of the clarity that made the company successful in the first place.

These outcomes would be bad enough on their own. But in the hyper-accelerated market conditions we're moving into, they're a death sentence. Companies that scale without maintaining adaptability will find themselves overtaken by smaller, faster-moving competitors who remain closer to PMF.

So, Market-Led Growth (MLG) rejects this approach entirely. Instead of assuming that growth must mean 'more of everything,' MLG companies view growth as a function of staying as close to PMF as possible at all times. Growth should never come at the expense of adaptability. It should never create friction between leadership and market responsiveness. It should never lead to the organization outgrowing its own ability to execute.

This is where fractal scaling comes in. It is the MLG alternative to traditional, linear scaling – a way for companies to expand without losing their speed, agility, or focus. To understand why it's helpful – indeed, necessary – we first need to explore what's wrong with the existing models of growth.

## Case study: PayPal's failure to split its consumer and merchant teams

PayPal was one of the first major players in online payments, originally gaining traction by powering peer-to-peer transactions for eBay sellers. At first, this gave them strong momentum in e-commerce payments. But instead of recognizing that business payments required a different GTM motion from consumer payments, PayPal continued treating all payments under one undifferentiated strategy.

PayPal didn't have a merchant-focused GTM that could tailor product features, pricing, and developer tools to e-commerce businesses. Instead, they continued applying the same payment infrastructure to both consumers and businesses. While they were treating merchants as just another PayPal user, Stripe (among others) was building a developer-first payments platform specifically for e-commerce.

Stripe's business-first approach resonated with startups, software-as-a-service (SaaS) companies, and e-commerce platforms. Instead of treating businesses as an afterthought, Stripe built for them from the ground up. By the time PayPal realized they needed a distinct merchant GTM motion, Stripe had already dominated the e-commerce space.

If PayPal had recognized early that consumer and business payments required different GTM motions, they could have created a dedicated pod for e-commerce merchants. That pod could have built tailored messaging, developer tools, and checkout flows specifically for online businesses. It wouldn't have been forced to make trade-offs between consumer and merchant needs, and most importantly, it would have protected PayPal's dominance in e-commerce before Stripe emerged.

Instead, they scaled as one large motion, assuming that what worked for consumers would work for businesses. That assumption gave Stripe the opportunity to build something better. This is why Fractal Scaling is necessary for the functioning of an MLG business.

## Fractal scaling: The MLG alternative to traditional growth

Fractal scaling ensures that even as an MLG company grows, it remains a network of small, highly focused, semi-autonomous pods, rather than a single, sprawling entity that slows itself down under its own weight. Each pod is that self-contained motion, optimized for a specific ICP, persona, or market segment that we described in Chapter 5.

While they all share infrastructure, best practices, and strategic alignment, each pod moves at its own pace, scaling based on real demand signals rather than arbitrary company-wide expansion goals. Instead of a single sales team growing until it becomes too broad to be effective, instead of a GTM motion expanding to cover more and more customer types until it loses its effectiveness, fractal scaling prevents bloat before it happens.

The key lies in what happens when you see success. Rather than expanding indefinitely, a pod that reaches a certain threshold doesn't get bigger – *it splits*.

- A team selling to CFOs doesn't scale by adding dozens of new sales reps. Instead, it spins off a second pod, with one team remaining focused on mid-market CFOs while another specializes in enterprise finance leaders.
- A GTM motion that works for U.S. buyers doesn't just assume the same playbook will work in Europe or Asia – it launches a new pod to validate that market separately.
- A team selling to subscription businesses doesn't expand into software-as-a-service (SaaS) and Media as if they were the same segment – it breaks apart into independent pods, each with a GTM strategy tailored to its specific ICP.

Each new pod inherits the learnings and successful execution model of the original, but instead of diluting focus, it refines it further. The original pod continues running what is already working, while the new pod explores how to optimize and expand into adjacent areas without breaking PMF.

This is a fundamental shift between traditional scaling and how MLG companies scale. In a traditional model, a successful GTM motion is scaled up, expanded, and extended until it becomes too complex to execute effectively, or ends up optimizing for only part of the now-overextended ICP (e.g., for the U.S. market, but not the Europe, the Middle East, and Africa (EMEA) market). In fractal scaling, success is met with a split – growth happens not by encouraging teams to get bigger, but by staying small, staying focused, and continuously refining PMF. The more successful you are, the more pods you can have, with tighter and tighter market-niches, ICPs, positioning and approaches.

## Staying small to grow big: How fractal scaling operates

One of the key reasons that traditional companies slow down as they scale is because teams grow too large to execute efficiently. The more people, budget, and scope a team accumulates, the harder it becomes to maintain focus, speed, and agility. Fractal scaling prevents this from happening by enforcing a simple rule: when a pod reaches a certain size or level of market complexity, it doesn't just keep growing – it splits.

### The Amazon approach

Amazon provides one of the best-known examples of this principle in action. Jeff Bezos implemented what is now known as the 'two-pizza team' rule – if a team can't be fed with two pizzas, it's too big. Instead of scaling a single team into a bloated, slow-moving department, Amazon splits teams when they hit complexity thresholds. This keeps execution fast, independent, and market-responsive, even as the company scales.

To maintain focus and accountability, Amazon employs 'single-threaded leaders' who are dedicated exclusively to one initiative or product. This leadership model ensures that each team has a clear vision and direction, free from competing priorities. These leaders are empowered to make decisions swiftly, fostering an environment where experimentation and calculated risk-taking are encouraged. This autonomy allows teams to pivot quickly based on customer feedback or market dynamics, embodying the essence of fractal scaling by enabling semi-independent growth and adaptation.

The same applies to fractal scaling. A pod focused on accountants might start as one motion, but once it reaches a certain size, it splits into separate pods for U.S. accountants, U.K. accountants, and EMEA accountants. By doing this, each pod can tailor its messaging, pricing, and GTM approach to its specific market without being weighed down by the needs of other regions.

The precise measure or threshold for when to preemptively split a pod is likely unique to each business. But the goal is simple: prevent teams from growing so large that they lose their ability to react to market shifts, or lose obsessive focus on a single ICP. By splitting early, teams can stay small, agile, and hyper-focused while still contributing to overall company growth. So, if you're extending a pod's focus into a new geography, or new persona, or new use-case, or new market, ask yourself – is this a new pod?

**Reminder**: This isn't a return to the general manager model. Fractal scaling doesn't create fully autonomous business units that operate independently from the company's core strategy. Instead, as we covered in Chapter 5, pods remain small, focused teams dedicated to refining ICP, GTM motion, messaging, and PMF. They execute within a shared framework, rather than setting their own rules for product, pricing, or overall strategy.

For example, the EMEA-focused pod we just described doesn't have to be physically based in EMEA – it simply ensures that the GTM approach for that market is optimized. It works within centrally defined guardrails for product, pricing, and sales infrastructure, but has the autonomy to refine messaging, positioning, and execution based on real market signals. The pod isn't deciding how EMEA as a whole should operate – it's focused on how best to engage and win in that specific market. Fractal scaling ensures that companies can scale with agility and precision without falling into the trap of fragmented, siloed decision-making.

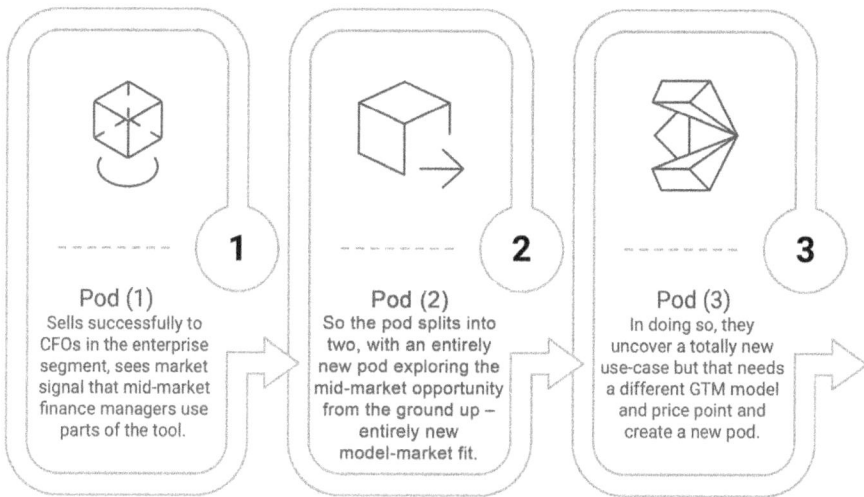

**Figure 21** Fractal scaling model. Fractal scaling keeps teams fast, focused, and responsive. When complexity creeps in, MLG pods split – preserving agility without losing alignment. Small teams scale better.

## Pods also split when PMF drifts

Fractal scaling isn't just about scaling what works – it's also about quickly diagnosing and fixing what's not working.

The overriding principle of MLG philosophy is the search for perpetual PMF. A GTM motion that was once successful may start to see declining win rates, rising customer acquisition costs (CAC), or slower deal cycles. When this happens, most companies try to fix the problem at the macro level – adjusting their pricing, tweaking their messaging, or increasing marketing spend across the board. But this approach often damages what's still working while failing to address the root cause of the issue.

Instead of applying broad, organization-wide changes, fractal scaling solves slowdown by splitting the pod that's experiencing PMF degradation. For example, a hypothetical SaaS company selling to CFOs might notice that its overall win rate is dropping. Instead of assuming the problem is company-wide, they segment their data and realize that CFOs in the U.S. are still converting at 30% (healthy

PMF). CFOs in EMEA have dropped to a 12% win rate (PMF is locally eroding).

Instead of making sweeping changes that might disrupt U.S. growth, the company splits the EMEA motion into its own pod. The U.S. team continues scaling as-is, while the EMEA team iterates on messaging, pricing, and GTM motion separately to find a better fit. By splitting, the company prevents a low-performing segment from dragging down the entire business while also creating a dedicated space to fix the problem without unnecessary disruption.

## A common mistake: Waiting too long to split

One of the most dangerous mistakes a company can make is to keep an underperforming segment within a high-performing pod and to hope it will self-correct. Market shifts rarely announce themselves in a single dramatic moment. Instead, PMF erosion happens gradually, and if it goes unchecked, it can quietly destabilize an entire business before anyone fully understands why.

If a once-successful ICP starts behaving differently – longer sales cycles, declining conversion rates, rising CAC – it's often a sign that the market has changed in a way that the existing motion is no longer optimized for.

The right response isn't to force a single team to adjust to two or more diverging ICPs – it's to split the underperforming segment into its own pod before it drags down the entire motion. If market complexity increases, and a single team is now serving customers with meaningfully different behaviors, needs, or buying processes, then waiting too long to split will only accelerate PMF degradation.

Go back to the previous example – If the pod focused on CFOs continues treating EMEA as just another part of its U.S. motion, it risks making adjustments that harm U.S. performance in an effort to 'fix' EMEA. Worse, leadership will naturally focus on the region where success is easiest, creating an even greater imbalance in targeting for the two regions.

By splitting the EMEA segment into its own pod, the company now has two independent teams, each with the autonomy to optimize for its specific market. The U.S. pod continues scaling its proven motion, while the EMEA pod can experiment with different positioning, pricing, or sales approaches without disrupting what's already working elsewhere.

Most companies wait until it's too late to make these changes. By the time leadership finally acknowledges the need for segmentation, PMF has eroded, teams are underperforming, and competitors have seized the opportunity to fill the gap. Fractal scaling ensures that splitting happens before PMF degradation spreads across the business. It prevents companies from making wholesale changes to their best-performing GTM motions simply because one segment is underperforming.

## When you can't find PMF, lose it for good

Not every pod will succeed. Some will struggle to find PMF from the start, never quite achieving a repeatable motion. Others may start strong but lose PMF over time as markets shift, competition increases, or buyer behavior changes. When this happens, companies face a critical decision: do you refine the pod further, collapse it back into another pod, or shut it down entirely?

A failing pod that remains operational becomes a slow bleed on resources, draining sales, marketing, and product attention away from areas of the business that are creating value. It also undermines the whole culture of the system – the process of learning, failure and growth.

The best MLG companies recognize that killing a pod isn't failure – it's discipline. Just as fractal scaling encourages companies to split pods early when markets start to diverge, it requires companies to merge or eliminate pods that no longer justify their existence. The challenge is: when should you do it?

The right decision depends on whether there is real evidence that further iteration will improve outcomes in an acceptable time period (does the company want to make a long-term bet, strategically?) or if the pod's focus is simply a poor fit for the company.

## The role of leadership in merging or shutting down pods

Just as leadership encourages pod splits when markets diverge, they also need to recognize when consolidation or shutdown is the best option. A well-functioning fractal scaling model ensures that pods exist only as long as they are needed.

- Collapsing pods back together isn't a step backward – it's a way to maintain efficiency when separate motions prove to be unnecessary.
- Shutting down a pod isn't an admission of failure – it's a demonstration of focus and discipline.

The best MLG companies operate with a clear framework for deciding when to refine, merge, or eliminate pods. They don't let struggling segments erode overall execution, and they prioritize maintaining agility over keeping every expansion attempt alive.

The goal of fractal scaling isn't just to create more pods – it's to ensure that every market motion is as precise and effective as possible. If that means merging or shutting down pods to stay focused on evolving PMF, that's a success – not a setback.

## Fractal scaling can seem inefficient – but it's what keeps you agile

At first glance, fractal scaling can seem inefficient. Instead of consolidating teams under one broad GTM motion, it deliberately creates smaller, focused pods that operate in parallel. Splitting pods requires more well-paid, highly skilled people running what in the short term might be near-identical GTM motions.

But this short-term inefficiency is what makes the company more adaptable in the long run. Instead of building a single, rigid structure that is difficult to change, fractal scaling ensures that businesses can continuously refine execution to stay close to PMF.

The payback comes in two ways. First, fractal scaling ensures that PMF is sustained or re-accelerated by allowing each pod to optimize for its specific segment, rather than forcing a single motion to work across different market conditions. This keeps execution sharp and aligned with real demand. Second, it enables faster iteration cycles that keep the company responsive to market shifts. Instead of requiring large-scale, company-wide changes that can slow execution, adjustments happen at the pod level, allowing for continuous refinement without disrupting the broader business.

The companies that scale the fastest often collapse under their own weight. They expand into too many markets too soon, stretching their GTM execution thin and losing sight of their strongest customers.

## Conclusion: Scaling isn't the goal – staying aligned to PMF is

A big error companies make is assuming that success means scaling everything at the same time. A team finds traction, a motion starts working, and suddenly leadership is making bold expansion plans: *'We've really got something here! Let's scale a team in the UK and Japan! Let's double our ad spend and reach all of EMEA!'* It's a common mistake – often exacerbated by venture capital (VC) funding models that push companies toward rapid expansion without ensuring the foundation is stable.

But in MLG, scaling isn't about growing for the sake of it – it's about staying as close as possible to evolving PMF. PMF isn't a static milestone that, once achieved, guarantees sustained success. It shifts constantly as markets mature, competition evolves, and customer needs change. The worst thing a company can do is scale so broadly and so quickly that it loses sight of where PMF is strongest.

Fractal scaling ensures that companies don't lose touch with PMF as they expand. Instead of treating growth as a uniform process, MLG companies scale based on where PMF is strongest and evolving most predictably.

- If a motion is validated, it scales aggressively – without waiting for other segments to catch up.
- If a motion is still being refined, it's given time to run several MLG cycles (sense, interpret, adapt, test) – without being forced into premature expansion.
- If a segment starts to struggle, it's split into its own pod – so it can adjust without distorting execution in high-PMF areas.

Scaling isn't the primary goal. Staying aligned with PMF is the primary goal. The companies that win aren't the ones that grow the fastest; they're the ones that scale without losing their ability to detect and respond to shifts in PMF. Fractal scaling ensures that growth remains a result of market alignment and execution excellence, not just an expectation.

# 13

# Beyond implementation: Risks, realities, and futures of growth

## Introduction: Everything changes everything

The shifts outlined so far – AI-native execution, decentralized pods, adaptive go-to-market (GTM), and continuous market sensing – aren't surface-level tactics. They change the operating system of a business, and when the operating system (OS) changes, so does everything it touches.

In this chapter, we step back from the mechanics of Market-Led Growth (MLG) to consider the ripple effects. What happens to org charts, capital allocation, the job market, pricing, brand, strategy – even the very nature of product itself – when the default assumptions of the last 20 years start to break? This isn't just a new playbook – it's a new terrain.

## Brand and relationships will become the last big differentiators

For now, speed is the advantage. The companies that execute faster, sense demand shifts earlier, and adapt in real time are the ones that win. However, that edge won't last forever.

Once every company is running some version of MLG, once real-time adaptation becomes the norm, speed alone won't be enough. A second-order effect of MLG becoming mainstream is that the playing field levels – everyone is fast, everyone is adaptive, everyone is AI-powered, and when that happens, the competitive advantage shifts to something else.

If AI can replicate features in weeks, if products begin to blur together in a sea of copy-and-paste, ever more fine-tuned pitches to ICPs, then buyers will no longer choose based on functionality alone. They'll choose based on familiarity, credibility, and confidence. They'll choose based on brand.

Brand has always mattered, but in a world where differentiation on product becomes razor-thin, it becomes essential. Buyers will default to the companies they already know, the ones they've heard of, the ones they feel are the safest bet. The business that tells the clearest, most compelling story will win, because every other factor being equal, people gravitate toward what feels certain.

Take Apple as an example. There are cheaper laptops, phones with better specs, and competitors that push updates faster. But Apple's brand gives them a gravitational pull that keeps customers locked in. When they launch a product, people assume it's the best – even before they compare specs, and in a world where AI can help competitors match their features almost instantly, that level of brand trust is the ultimate moat.

Brand alone, however, won't be enough. The irony of an AI-driven market is that human relationships become more valuable, not less. For all the efficiencies AI enables, for all the personalization algorithms can deliver, there is still something irreplaceable about a real connection between a company and its customers. When automation reaches its peak, the human touch will be one of the last big differentiators.

- Customer service, support, and personalization will matter more than ever. The experience of working with a company – the way they engage, respond, and adapt to customer needs – will be just as important as the product itself.
- In high-value markets, people still buy from other people. AI may optimize outreach, but relationships will drive retention, expansion, and advocacy.

- Long-term trust will outweigh short-term optimization. The companies that treat customers as partners, rather than transactions, will build resilience that AI-driven automation alone cannot provide.

*AI will make execution more efficient. But human connection will give companies staying power.*

## The nature of moats is changing, threatening retention assumptions

In knowledge work today, defensibility often rests on friction. Clients and customers don't just buy a service or subscribe to a platform – they become entangled in it. Processes are tailored. Outputs are non-standard. Workflows embed themselves across teams and systems. Over time, even average solutions become difficult to unwind. The deeper the integration, the harder the exit.

This is not accidental, it's how advantage is currently constructed. Switching costs create stickiness. In enterprise software, long implementations and custom configurations discourage movement. In legal or financial services, institutional memory and contract entanglement keep clients in place. In consulting, reputation and embedded ways of working act as soft deterrents to change. These moats are not about product or performance. They are about the pain of leaving.

But this dynamic is starting to break down. AI tools don't just accelerate productivity – they remove the glue. AI can translate contracts, map APIs, generate alternative workflows, and reconstruct outputs in new formats. What used to take weeks of human coordination can now happen through intelligent agents in hours. In some domains, an entire system of work can be duplicated or redesigned with a prompt.

Salesforce illustrates the shift. For years, its strength has been not just functionality, but entrenchment. Customers built on it. Partners built around it. Over time, migrating away became unthinkable – not because Salesforce was universally loved, but because the effort required to leave felt insurmountable. That logic is weakening. With AI tools that automate schema migration, rebuild interfaces, and orchestrate integrations, the structural advantage of that entrenchment is fading. Salesforce's depth once protected it. Now it risks becoming ballast.

This pattern is emerging everywhere. Law firms face generative tools that draft and review contracts in minutes. Strategic advisors compete with models that synthesize research, simulate outcomes, and suggest actions. Wealth managers lose ground to automated platforms that personalize portfolios in real time. In each case, the foundation of retention is under pressure – not because the service is worse, but because staying no longer feels safer than switching.

Moats still matter. But their foundations are shifting – from institutional friction to adaptive capability. The future belongs to firms that evolve in step with their clients. That respond faster than others can catch up. When leaving is easy, the only true moat is being providing value worth staying for.

## Pricing and monetization will become more fluid

Pricing has long been one of the most rigid aspects of GTM strategy. For decades, businesses have operated on fixed pricing structures – tiers, contracts, and standard discounting models, all set in place and reviewed once or twice a year. But just as MLG has made GTM execution more adaptive, pricing models are beginning to follow suit.

We have entered a world where pricing is no longer static, but dynamic – where it flexes in real time based on demand, competition, and customer behavior. Companies that once set their pricing in stone find themselves struggling to compete with those that treat pricing as a live, strategic lever. This shift isn't just about offering personalized discounts or regional pricing adjustments. It's something far bigger: AI-driven, one-to-one pricing optimization.

Pricing won't just be customized by segment, it will be personalized at an individual level. AI will analyze buying signals, industry trends, and competitive data to recommend the right pricing structure for each customer at any given moment. For some buyers, that may mean usage-based models that scale with their needs. For others, it may mean outcome-based pricing, where they pay for results rather than a fixed subscription.

As AI gets smarter, fixed pricing will start to feel outdated. The days of rigid plans with little flexibility will give way to dynamic, real-time pricing that adapts to market shifts on the fly. Companies that can execute this well will capture revenue more efficiently, ensuring that pricing always reflects the true value a customer perceives.

But there's a fine line between adaptability and chaos. If pricing changes too frequently, buyers will lose confidence. No one wants to feel like they're being manipulated, or that pricing is inconsistent from one moment to the next. The challenge will be in striking the right balance – adapting pricing without undermining trust.

Look at Airbnb as an example. In its early days, pricing was simple: hosts set a rate, and guests either booked or they didn't. Today, Airbnb's AI-powered pricing engine continuously adjusts rates based on demand, seasonality, competitor listings, and even booking patterns.

That same shift is coming for B2B software-as-a-service (SaaS), enterprise software, and service-based businesses. Companies locked into static pricing structures will find themselves losing deals to competitors who can adjust on the fly, capturing value more effectively.

The real winners in this shift won't just be those that move to dynamic pricing – it will be those that do so transparently, fairly, and with a deep understanding of how to build trust while optimizing revenue. In a world where market conditions change by the day, pricing must change with them.

## The war for AI talent will expand beyond R&D

The war for AI talent is already well underway. Microsoft, Google, Meta, OpenAI – these companies are paying millions to secure the best machine learning engineers and data scientists. They understand that AI execution is now a direct determinant of business success. But what happens when AI becomes embedded not just in R&D, but in every function of the business?

As companies adopt MLG principles, the demand for AI-driven adaptability will spread far beyond the traditional AI research teams. It won't just be about hiring machine learning engineers – it will be about transforming the kind of talent businesses look for across sales, marketing, product, and GTM execution.

This shift is already beginning. The most forward-thinking companies are starting to look for a new kind of professional – one who isn't just a hyper-specialist in a single domain, but who can operate at the intersection of AI, strategy, and execution.

- The line between software engineer and marketer will blur. As AI plays a larger role in demand generation, marketing teams won't just need creative thinkers – they will need people who understand data, algorithms, and how to optimize AI-driven execution in real time. The best marketers of the future will be just as comfortable working alongside machine learning models as they are crafting positioning and messaging.
- Salespeople will need to think like strategists. In an MLG-driven world, the best sales reps won't just be relationship managers or deal-closers – they'll be market intelligence operators, leveraging AI-driven insights to refine positioning, spot demand shifts, and dynamically adapt their sales approach.
- GTM teams will become more fluid and cross-functional. The days of rigid silos between product, marketing, and sales will start to break down. Companies will need people who can move across functions, understanding how AI impacts every part of the revenue engine and adapting execution in real time.

The companies that recognize this shift early will redesign hiring and development around adaptability. They will look for talent that isn't just experienced in traditional marketing, sales, or product – but people who can think in a system-wide way, using AI-driven insights to guide execution across multiple domains. It will be about reshaping the kind of people businesses hire at every level – favoring adaptability over narrow specialization, execution speed over rigid expertise, and AI fluency over traditional experience.

## The end of the expertise pyramid

This evolution isn't limited to tech companies or GTM teams. It's already shaking the foundations of expertise-based businesses – law firms, consultancies, accountancies – where headcount has long been structured as a pyramid. Each year, firms hire large classes of juniors, who grind through long hours and narrow tasks in the hopes of one day becoming partner. The economics depend on volume: lots of juniors doing billable work that funds the top.

But that model is starting to break. AI doesn't just augment knowledge work – it mechanizes cognition. Research, synthesis, templating, modelling – tasks that once filled junior calendars – can increasingly be done better, faster, and cheaper by machines. Some junior staff will still be needed, but fewer. The funnel narrows, the ladder shortens, and the case for the pyramid starts to collapse.

If capital, scale, and efficiency no longer reinforce each other, why stay in the structure at all? What's to stop a senior partner from leaving, hiring a small team, and building a high-leverage boutique with better economics and more autonomy? The overhead of the traditional firm becomes a drag, not an asset. The brand becomes a nice-to-have, not a moat.

There's a deeper challenge – if fewer juniors are hired, who replaces the seniors when they retire? Are we heading toward smaller, faster, more disposable firms – without a talent pipeline? Or will large firms double down on their brand, becoming more like aggregators and less like training grounds? Either way, the disaggregation of expertise is underway, and once it starts, it's hard to reverse.

# Funding models will have to change

The execution model has changed, but the funding model has not. Venture capital and private equity remain the two dominant mechanisms through which growth-stage businesses are financed. Both are optimized for companies that plan their growth trajectory in advance, raise capital in bulk, and execute against a fixed set of assumptions. That logic no longer holds. In a world where execution must adapt constantly to live market signals, the existing capital structures no longer fit.

This isn't just a philosophical mismatch, it's operational. MLG depends on a company's ability to reallocate resources at speed – to test, respond, and evolve with demand. But most businesses are still capitalized by investors who expect pre-committed spend, linear progression, and milestone-based returns. As more companies begin to operate with MLG principles, this friction will become unsustainable.

The implication is clear: funding models will have to change. Capital will need to be structured not as a bet on a plan, but as a system that flexes with execution. The infrastructure of investment – how capital is deployed, how success is defined, how risk is managed – must evolve to support adaptive operating models, not constrain them.

## The incompatibility of today's structures

Venture capital forces companies into a high-stakes trajectory. The assumption is that winners will deliver outlier returns, so growth must be rapid, expansive, and often premature. Once capital is raised, spend is expected. Forecasts become commitments. Plans ossify. Changing direction – even when the market demands it – risks investor confidence and valuation resets. For MLG companies, this logic is untenable. You cannot run a sensing-and-response system on a 24-month pre-approved burn plan.

Private equity imposes a different, but equally limiting, constraint. The model optimizes for predictable returns through operational efficiency, cost discipline, and tightly managed budgets. Reinvestment is difficult. Adaptation is often deprioritized. Even when market conditions shift, the system resists change. In the language of MLG, private equity (PE) structures assume the GTM motion is fixed, and all that remains is to refine it. But when product-market fit is fluid, efficiency without flexibility is fragility.

These are not minor problems. As execution becomes more adaptive, companies funded through traditional venture capital (VC) or PE will increasingly find themselves unable to act on market signals – because their capital structure prevents it. The more dynamic the operating model becomes, the more static the financing model feels by comparison.

## The future of capital deployment must be dynamic

What's required now is not a new funding ideology, but a new funding mechanism – one that treats capital as something deployed in motion, not in bulk. The future of financing will be defined by structures that support responsiveness, not rigidity.

This potentially means a shift away from single-shot fundraising events and toward rolling capital access models – committed pools of capital released incrementally based on validated progress, not time-bound projections. Think of it as *Just-In-Time Funding*: investors underwrite the team and thesis, but release capital in phases, tied to real traction, learning, and fit. The result is a system that adapts with the company, rather than forcing the company to iterate its earliest assumptions.

In private equity, the equivalent may be dynamic reallocation models – zero-based budgets that reset every quarter, combined with fluid performance thresholds that permit reinvestment when opportunity emerges. Rather than forcing companies to optimize toward a static profit and loss (P&L), this model would allow them to chase demand – so long as the returns on capital justify the reallocation.

Neither of these models is common today, but both are coming. As MLG adoption grows, the companies that win will be those that can move capital with the same agility they move GTM resources. The investors who back them will be those who understand that optionality is the most valuable asset a company can have in emerging market conditions.

## The role of investors will evolve

This shift isn't just operational, it's cultural. Capital partners will need to think less like financial engineers and more like systems designers. They will be judged not just on their ability to pick winners, but on their ability to architect funding systems that support continuous adaptation. The limited partner–general partner relationship will need to evolve accordingly, with fund structures that accommodate more variable timelines, distributed outcomes, and flexible return profiles.

Monitoring will change too – board meetings can no longer be reviews of variance to plan – they must become assessments of executional adaptability. The question will not be 'did we hit the forecast?' but 'did we respond fast enough when the forecast broke?' This shift requires a different rhythm, different metrics, and a different mindset. It rewards learning velocity over milestone completion. It values market alignment over internal consistency.

In many ways, this future returns capital to its first principles. The job of capital is not to enforce discipline through rigidity. It is to enable a team to pursue the best version of the opportunity in front of them – and to adapt when that opportunity changes shape. In MLG, that change is constant. The funding model must be just as fluid.

### This book doesn't offer a financial blueprint – but it names the problem

This is not a capital markets playbook, it is a handbook for execution. But no execution model can scale sustainably if its financial foundation locks it into the past. MLG is forcing a redefinition of what it means to fund growth. It is not enough to invest in innovation at the product level. Innovation must extend to how companies are capitalized, measured, and supported as they scale.

That change will not happen all at once, but the direction is clear. Capital will have to move from forecast to feedback, from pre-allocation to dynamic flow, from spreadsheet-driven control to signal-driven support. Investors who recognize this shift early will gain access to the most resilient and adaptive businesses of the next decade. Those who don't will be left trying to impose outdated control systems on companies built to outgrow them.

## The concept of a 'product' is becoming obsolete

In most of modern business, a product has been a stable unit of value. It was built, packaged, priced, and sold. Customers adapted to the product, not the other way around. Companies iterated cautiously, launching updates via controlled cycles – monthly, quarterly, annually – guarded by roadmaps and release schedules. Even in the cloud era, the mental model of the product as a discrete, finished thing has persisted.

But in an MLG environment, that framing collapses. When customer needs are volatile and organizations are structured for continuous sensing and execution, the product itself can no longer remain fixed – it becomes porous. real-time, reflexive.

This is not a metaphor, it is a shift in business physics. The combination of real-time data, AI-driven analysis, and adaptive execution allows the product to become a *living interface* between company capability and market need. It is not a static object. It is a process – an ongoing negotiation between what the company can do and what the market is asking for.

Consider what's already happening:

- **Amazon Web Services** doesn't sell boxed software. It offers composable capabilities – compute, storage, security – that customers assemble and pay for based on actual usage. Pricing, availability, and features are adjusted constantly. AWS's 'product' is better understood as a living ecosystem, tuned continuously to customer signal.
- **Tesla** treats its vehicles less like fixed hardware and more like software platforms. Over-the-air updates change functionality post-sale – upgrading battery performance, adjusting braking systems, even adding entirely new features like in-car entertainment. Your Tesla at delivery is not your Tesla six months later.
- **Spotify** doesn't ship a product so much as choreograph a continuous experience. Algorithms adapt playlists in real time. New features, partnerships, and experiments roll out constantly to test engagement and improve retention. The 'product' is closer to a probabilistic engine of relevance than a fixed feature set.
- **Figma** evolved not just through feature releases but through live customer usage. Its collaborative model allowed real-time learning from user interaction. What began as a design tool became a broader coordination platform, precisely because the team viewed product boundaries as permeable and shaped by behavior.

## These examples are not edge cases: They are signals of a deeper pattern

As more companies embrace adaptive infrastructure and AI-native execution, we should expect 'product' to become a second-order concept. The unit of value shifts from the product *itself* to the system that configures and delivers it *in response to market dynamics*. This shift reshapes how companies operate on multiple levels:

1.  **Features become optional**: Rather than gating value behind SKUs, companies begin to blur the lines between product, service, and platform. Users unlock capabilities as they need them, and the system adjusts to optimize value delivery dynamically.

2.  **Roadmaps become probabilistic**: The role of product management evolves. It's no longer just about prioritizing features for future releases – it's about orchestrating experiments, interpreting signal, and governing the systems that adapt in real time.

3.  **Customers become co-creators**: Adaptive systems can learn from individual behavior, but also from patterns across users. In this way, the product evolves not from internal strategy alone, but from a collective dialogue with the market.

4.  **Support, success, and product blend**: When the product is no longer fixed, the traditional silos between product, customer success, and support begin to erode. Each touchpoint becomes an opportunity for the system to learn and adjust.

## What comes after the product?

This raises a provocative question: If product as a category dissolves, what takes its place? I am speculating here, but the logic leads us somewhere interesting. It may be that *systems* replace products as the primary unit of value creation. Companies stop thinking in terms of delivering 'solutions' and start thinking in terms of deploying *adaptive surfaces* – responsive layers that shape themselves around customer needs.

Think of Netflix. Is it a product? A service? A brand? A distribution platform? It doesn't matter. What matters is that it functions as a continuously evolving interface to stories. The more it learns from you, the more precisely it tunes its offerings. The boundaries of 'product' melt away.

In a similar vein, consider OpenAI's ChatGPT. What version are you using? What does it include? You likely don't know – or care. You care about the outcome, and that outcome is continuously shifting based on signal from millions of users. What's delivered to you is mediated by a learning system, not a roadmap. You aren't buying features, you're entering into a feedback loop.

This reframing has implications well beyond technology. It challenges the legal concept of a product. It undermines fixed pricing and procurement processes. It stretches operational, ethical, and regulatory frameworks built for a world of objects, not systems. It also calls into question the very structure of the firm.

If the product is fluid the organization that builds it must be too. You cannot operate a reflexive system through a fixed hierarchy. You need decentralized sensing, fast decision cycles, modular teams. You need an operating model built not on control but on learning – precisely the shift we've described throughout this book.

## Adapt or fossilize

None of this is speculative in the sense of 'maybe someday.' It's already happening at the frontier. The only speculation is how far, and how fast, it will go. The more capable your sensing systems, and the more autonomous your execution loops, the less sense it makes to treat the product as a fixed noun.

In the long run, the companies that thrive won't be those with the best static offerings. They'll be those with the most adaptive surfaces – systems that absorb signal, configure capability, and deliver value in real time. If that sounds abstract, that's only because we're still clinging to industrial-era metaphors. But make no mistake: I believe we are watching the end of the product age.

# Afterword: A letter to you, dear reader

If you've made it this far – thank you. That's no small thing. You've just read a book that doesn't promise a hack, a shortcut, or a magic metric. What it does offer is a way of seeing: a new lens for understanding how growth works in an economy that no longer plays by the rules many of us built our careers around, and that nearly every successful business was built to take advantage of.

I didn't write this book because I think the old ways were stupid. I wrote it because I think the world has changed faster than our operating models have. Sales-Led Growth and Product-Led Growth worked – for a time. But they were built for a different market: centralized demand, cheap capital, and execution cycles measured in quarters. That world is gone, and most companies are still trying to run last decade's playbooks on this decade's terrain.

AI is rewriting some of the fundamental rules of business – just as the last industrial revolution redefined economies and labor structures. But adaptation doesn't mean throwing out every principle that came before it. The core tenets of economics remain: markets still operate on supply and demand, capital must still be allocated wisely, and businesses must still deliver value that customers are willing to pay for.

In other words, death, taxes, and Shark Week on the Discovery Channel remain inevitable. The difference between yesterday and tomorrow is that everything moves faster, cycles are compressed, and existing competitive advantages evaporate at unprecedented speeds.

Market-Led Growth (MLG) isn't a new flavor of go-to-market (GTM). It's an attempt to rewire how companies operate – strategically, structurally, and culturally – so they can adapt continuously, rather than react belatedly. It's a framework for reflex. A loop, not a line. One that starts with signal, turns it into action without delay, learns in real time, and scales only what stays aligned with fit.

This book is not a manual, it's a provocation. A challenge to drop the illusion that leadership is about certainty, or that strategy is something you do annually. The MLG model doesn't just decentralize execution – it redefines leadership. It treats capital not as a plan to follow but as a resource to steer dynamically. It puts customers – not personas, not segments, but the live, moving market – at the center of the system, and it uses AI not as a tool to speed up the old ways, but as a substrate for building entirely new ones.

It's tempting to see MLG as an upgrade, but it's more like a reinstallation. You're not adding a layer – you're switching operating systems.

None of this is easy. Building fast reflexes means letting go of control. Delegating authority means tolerating mess. Moving at speed means making mistakes – and learning faster than the cost of those mistakes – compound. MLG doesn't protect you from failure. But it does make your failures cheaper, your wins more repeatable, and your organization more alive to what's changing outside the building.

If this book has worked, it has done one thing: helped you see that reflex is not just a function of good tools or agile teams, it is a function of how you build, how you lead, and how willing you are to act on what the market is telling you – even when it's inconvenient.

The future doesn't reward optimization, it rewards alignment, and the organizations that survive the next era of business won't be the ones with the most scale, the best funding, or the strongest legacy. They'll be the ones with the fewest excuses for inaction.

MLG isn't a silver bullet. It's just the best way I know to meet a moving market with a system built to move. I wish you way more than luck. The rest is up to you.

This is the way.

**Felix**

# Index

www.ingramcontent.com/pod-product-compliance
Lightning Source LLC
Chambersburg PA
CBHW021920190326
41519CB00009B/858